FEATURING TRIPS ON: STAFFA, SOUTHERN MULL, AND THE WESTERN HIGHLANDS OF SCOTLAND

ROCKS
on wheels

GUIDES TO
SCOTLAND'S
ROAD ACCESSIBLE
GEOLOGY

CORLANN GEE BUSH AND KATIE L. GEE
SCOTTISH SOCIETY OF MOBILE, ALABAMA, USA

ROCKS ON WHEELS
Guides to Scotland's Road Accessible Geology

iUniverse books may be ordered through booksellers or by contacting:

iUniverse
1663 Liberty Drive
Bloomington, IN 47403
www.iuniverse.com
1-800-Authors (1-800-288-4677)

Because of the dynamic nature of the Internet, any web addresses or links contained in this book may have changed since publication and may no longer be valid. The views expressed in this work are solely those of the author and do not necessarily reflect the views of the publisher, and the publisher hereby disclaims any responsibility for them.

Any people depicted in stock imagery provided by Getty Images are models, and such images are being used for illustrative purposes only.
Certain stock imagery © Getty Images.

ISBN: 978-1-5320-7776-0 (sc)
ISBN: 978-1-5320-7777-7 (e)

Library of Congress Control Number: 2019908585

Print information available on the last page.

iUniverse rev. date: 06/29/2019

Contents

ORIENTATION v

KATIE'S SAFETY RULES xi

TRIP GUIDES:

TRIP 1 (SFA): There and Back Again : Staffa and Fingal's Cave 1

TRIP 2 (MUL): *Mulling It Over* : Southern Mull 17

TRIP 3 (UIN): *Through Eternity to Time* : Ullapool to Inchnadamph 38

TRIP 4 (LAS): *Soul Finding Country* : Loch Assynt..................................... 58

TRIP 5 (UNK): *Between Rocks and Reason* : Unapool to Keodale..........................72

TRIP 6. (KDC): ....*The More Things Change, The More They Change* : The Kyle of Durness to Smoo Cave 89

EPILOGUE: *Hail and Farewell!*: The Ceannabeinne Overlooks 106

BIBLIOGRAPHY 111

ORIENTATION

This Guide is for you if you have an interest in understanding the geology want to be more than an "accidental tourist" and learn the geological story behind some of the scenery you will see as you walk on Staffa and drive across southern Mull and the Northwest Highlands of Scotland. We have selected six different, geologically significant sites (we call them "Stops") on six different road trips that you are likely to take.

The Scotland has rightly been called a "Mecca" for geologists, and the Scottish government takes this honor seriously. Scottish Natural Heritage has published **Scotland: The Creation of its Natural Landscape: A Landscape Fashioned by Geology.** This excellent resource is free and available (as far as we know) at bookstores and tourist information centers-what few remain- throughout Scotland and at: pubs@snh.gov. uk. This publication contains information, maps, and illustrations about the geology of Scotland we cannot begin to replicate in this Guide. So we want you to get a copy because we will refer to it throughout this Guide.

In addition, many excursion guides and field trip logs, similar to this, have been developed to both geologists and geotourists. The best of these, relevant to the areas discussed in this Guide, are: Goodenough and Krabbendam's **A Geological Excursion Guide to the North-West Highlands of Scotland** (2010) and Strachan's **An Excursion Guide to the Moine** (2010). These have been written for professional geologists and serious students of geology. There are also abundant resources for people who want generalized information about the geology of specific areas. These include: the **Rock**

Route stops and displays, the **Pebble Route** pamphlets, the **North Coast 500**, and John Roberts' **Highland Trail Geology Guide.**

So you might be thinking: "given all these resources, why write another geology guide?" There are several reasons. First, and most important, we wanted to introduce you to some of the most important geo-sites in the world and explain them to you in easy to understand but not over-simplified terms. Second, we wanted to mix roadside sites that are famous (they would pull our geo-tour writers license for malpractice if we didn't) with others that are much less well known (Cat Scratch Fever, for example). So, we have "split the difference" by simplifying the technical information intended for professional audiences available in the "Geological Excursion Guides" and expanding on the information presented on the roadside informational panels and displays. Third, we did not want to complicate the six sites by adding relatively difficult to understand features like geological cross sections. But, if you are interested, the best cross section of the rocks of the Highlands you will be encountering on Trips 3, 4 and 5 is Callan Bentley's at: *earthmagazine.org.*

We realize that you are probably visiting Scotland for a brief period of time and, as unlikely as it seems to Corky, you may have other things you want to do besides learn about its geology. So, we have focused this Guide on the geology you can see near the roads while driving (five) and walking (one) well travelled routes, herein called "**Trips.**" And, to help you achieve the goal of seeing and understanding the unique geology that is here while still leaving time for other things such as eating, shopping, talking, we have limited the "**Stops**" to six per trip. Finally, in writing ***Rocks on Wheels***, we have made some assumptions about **you**. First, while you may have taken a geology or Earth Science course in high school or college, you have not had much acquaintance with the subject since then, except for watching occasional National Geographic specials. Second, you have taken the ferry to Staffa and/or you have rented a car and are driving yourself through Mull and the Highlands and can, within reason, set your own schedule. Thus, you can stop and look at geological features without, as they say, "missing the bus."

Caveats:

1. We sometimes cite information from Wikipedia. As you know, "Wiki" is the modern day **Encyclopedia Britannica,** except it does not collapse our bookshelves! But, as wonderful as it is, Wiki is impossible to keep up with! Wiki entries can change over hours, days and weeks as opposed to the years it took to update an entry in a print encyclopedia. So, if we do cite, quote or reference a Wiki entry, we give you the date we accessed that entry. But be aware that much may have changed since then! We apologize in advance for giving you wrong search terms or references to dead entries.

2. Since Wiki entries are usually "crowd sourced" rather than written and edited exclusively by acknowledged experts in a field, as print encyclopedias were, there is no one who ensures that a WIKI entry is as "correct" as possible or checks to ensure that different articles on the same or closely related subjects are not internally contradictory. For these reasons, even if we do refer you to a Wiki article, we will, by and large, not quote it. You can read it and related material for yourself. And we urge you to do so.

3. Technology is changing access to information and illustrations of that information faster than this Guide can be typed, edited and posted. We know we have made errors and apologize for them in advance! Please bring them to our attention so we can correct errors in future editions of RxOW. We will try to make corrections on line if you bring errors to our attention. Corky's email address is: corkyb43@yahoo.com.

4. No road or access information written in a Guide like this can be certain for more than five minutes after we write it! Map coordinates (location information) obtained from different sources can and does disagree. Odometers on cars can vary wildly, meaning that the mileage we give you to a site can be off by, well, a lot. Weather and road construction can change driving routes. Access to a site may be closed. Entrances are moved. A turn off or pull out that is clearly visible from one direction may be obscured from the other. We try to give you the most relevant and accurate information about how to access a site as we can. And we will be wrong. We apologize for these problems and errors in advance. If you point them out to us, we will try to correct or update this Guide as we can.

5. There is one way in which things in Scotland have not changed over the last decade we have visited: **<u>Scotland's roads are dangerous!</u>** In the summer, there are too many cars going too fast on narrow, mostly one lane, roads. For drivers from Canada and the US, everything is switched around. You must remember: **Drive Left; Look Right** because not all roads and intersections are well marked.

And since many of the **Stops** presented in this Guide, except those on Staffa, involve you and probably others getting out of your car and walking, you must be extra cautious when doing this! Katie's excellent road safety rules follow. Please read them now and review them every morning before starting out on that day's adventure.

6. The Scottish Outdoor Access Code is available at **outdooraccess-scotland.com.**

7. We visit Scotland, we do not live here. Things change, and we will likely be completely unaware of those changes, as happened this year with the change of location of stop near Elphin. So, when we are wrong about something like a route to or from the location of a feature, which we hope will not be often, please try to be flexible and forgiving! And let us know about the change at <u>corkyb43@yahoo.com</u> so we can try to correct the error.

We realize that all these caveats and expectations are a lot to process, but you need to know them! And the best time to tell you is at the beginning of your trip. Thank You!

We are: Geologist and Author: Corlann Gee Bush [corkyb43@yahoo.com]

Photographer/Driver: Katie Gee [saintedwes@gmail.com].

Executive Assistant: Christina Head [christinaLhead@gmail.com]

Sponsor: Scottish Society of Mobile, AL [Scottishsocietyofmobile.org].

Katie's Safety Rules

✓ Many roads, particularly in the Highlands, are single track with frequent, if unannounced, passing places you can swerve into to let cars pass. These are not parking places and you should not stop in them.

✓ There are also wider spots along the road into which you can pull and stop your car. If you do this, be sure to pull as far off the roadway as possible.

✓ On single track roads, it is usually the driver of the first car to reach a pull off or wide spot who is expected to pull in and wait for oncoming cars to pass by.

✓ Even if you plan to stay in the car while looking at a feature, set your handbrake and turn on your flashers.

✓ Pre-teen children should stay in the car unless we indicate that a site or parking area is large enough and safe enough that children can get out and see the feature being discussed. (Unfortunately, there are not many of these.)

✓ You and every member of your party should wear bright, protective clothing when leaving your car to look at an outcrop or feature. "Lovely," greenish yellow, 'hi-viz' vests are for sale at the Rock Shop near Kylescu, at many charity shops in Scotland's larger cities and towns, and at other stores around the Highlands. (These vests are not included in your car rental package, although they should be!)

✓ Carry a walking stick whenever you leave the car. You will use this for everything from helping yourself over puddles to showing the scale of a geological feature to you want to photograph.

✓ **Listen** for oncoming traffic. The roads in Scotland are curvy and hilly so you are more likely to hear an approaching vehicle that to see it.

✓ Only one person at a time should cross a road, study a feature, collect samples, or take pictures. Others should watch for traffic and warn of hazards such as falling rocks and speeding cars.

✓ Don't climb up or across any outcrop. You can see everything you need to see from the roadside or the pull off.

Finally, you must observe the following outdoor **conduct expectations**:

1. No hammering on outcrops to collect a sample or to break a large rock into smaller pieces. There are almost always pieces of rock lying along the roadside or at the base of the outcrop that you can pick up without endangering yourself or harming the outcrop or feature.

2. If you must take a rock sample home with you, take only ONE per group, not one sample for each member of the group! And be sure to label it with the name of what you believe the sample to be, and where and when you collected it. (Corky has received strange looks from Customs Officer, but has been able to bring small rocks aboard planes.)

3. Remember that pictures are worth a thousand words and several pounds of rock. If you must take home a rock sample, label it with the date and location you collected it and what you think it is. Then wrap it in tissue or cloth. Rock samples are surprisingly delicate for being made of, well, rock.

4. Have a wonderful time!!!! We want your use of this Guide to enhance your visit to this wonderfully historically, culturally, and geologically rich country!

If you get lost, the local livestock is always glad to point the way to the outcrops!

TRIP 1
There...and Back Again
(Rocks on "Heels")
A Walker's Guide to the Geology
Staffa and Fingal's Cave
(SFA)

The Island of Staffa is a "must see" for every tourist visiting Scotland. Here are six sights you **must see** while you're here.

CONTENTS

Caveats, Special Information, and Helpful Hints

SFA-1: *Here Comes Da Fudge*: Some Characteristics of Basalts
SFA-2: *We Just Want to Go with the Flow*: Hot Lavas and "Cool" Basalts
SFA-3: *Things Are Tuff All Over*: Igneous Rocks of the Air
SFA-4: *"Through Caverns Measureless"*: Fingal's Cave
SFA-5: *'Chill, Dude! Don't Be Such a Skerry'*: The Herdsman and His Islets
SFA-6: *'Fin'agling' the Truth*: MacCool's "Giant" Web of Lies Exposed--(A brief, personal essay by Corky)

CAVEATS, SPECIAL INFORMATION, and HELPFUL HINTS.

Most of the observations presented under the designations SFA-1, SFA-2, etc. can be made at several different places as you walk the island. If this is not the case, specific directions are given to help you find or see the specific feature discussed.

This Section of the Guide begins and ends at the boat landing on the island of Staffa. The only way to get to Staffa is by boat. You are expected to be back at the boat when it sails-- which is usually no more than an hour after landing. Since there is a lot to see on this amazing island and so little time to see it, consider taking the morning sailing and negotiating to return on the afternoon sailing. (Note: You must do this in advance!) If you cannot schedule more time on the island, you will probably not be able to see all the features discussed below, spend some quality time in Fingal's Cave, **and** see the puffin colony in that hour. Even if you are able to negotiate a morning arrival and an afternoon return, you will still need to budget your time. Also, the island is not handicapped accessible. You should discuss any mobility issues with the tour operator before booking your trip. And you must bring with you, and take away, anything you think you will need while there **including water and a lunch**.

Basalt is very slippery when it's wet, and even when it isn't. Walking on the island can be difficult because the rocks and pathways are slippery. For this reason, we recommend that you carry a walking stick, wear thick soled, tie shoes or boots, and walk with a partner.

Finally, there are no facilities on the island. Not just no souvenir shops, no ice cream trucks and no soda dispensers, but no facilities of any sort—anywhere. If you book on the ship the "Iolaire" from Fionnphort, there is a head (toilet) on board. But if you take the morning boat to Staffa and the afternoon sailing to return, you will need to plan "ahead." (Sorry for the pun.) If you do not sail on the Iolaire, you should ask about lavatory facilities before booking. (Now you know why stays on Staffa last only an hour and the public toilets on Iona and Fionnphort are so close to the jetties.)

SFA-1: *Here Comes Da Fudge!* : Some Characteristics of Basalts.

The entire island of Staffa is composed of *basalt* from just one flow that occurred approximately 60 million years ago. Photo SFA-1 shows the southern end of the island with Fingal's Cave and the three "zones" that developed as the lava cooled into basalt. These are:

(A) a top zone of small columns,

(B) a thick middle zone of rubbly, unformed columns, and

(c) a bottom layer of large, vertical well formed columns.

You can see this differentiation in the following photo of Staffa.

SFA-1: View of the southern end of Staffa, showing the entrance to Fingal's Cave, the columns, and the "atypical" zoning of the basalts.

Most basalts do not "cool" from lava in this way. The normal sequence of lava cooling into basalt is:

(a) a top zone of scoria and poorly developed columns,

(b) a middle zone of well formed, vertical columns, and

(c) a bottom section of rubbly, poorly formed columns.

The fact that the profile of the Staffa basalts does not conform to the typical basalt profile tells us that something out of the ordinary--for basalts--occurred here. So, let's break that down! **Basalt** is an igneous rock that forms when lava flows out onto or near the surface of the earth and cools "quickly." (The word "quickly" as used in geology, is a relative term because very few things happen very fast. Here it means "cooling faster than granite.")

The basalts on Staffa are atypical in more than just their "cooling profile": they were actually intruded into one large deposit of *tuff*, and the flow never broke out onto the surface of the earth. Tuff is windblown ash. The deposit was hundreds of feet thick, and the lava flowed within the tuff, forming what geologists call a **sill**. (A sill flows within or along an already existing rock unit; a dike flows across one.) Later, after the bottom and top layers of the flow had cooled but before the center of the sill had cooled, "something" came along and "jostled" the cooling lavas, interrupting column formation in the middle zone of the flow.

The Staffa flow was one of hundreds of flows that erupted over thousands of years and covered, collectively, an area that extended from Scotland as far south as what is now Ireland and as far west as what is now Greenland. Geologists use the term *flood basalts* to describe flows that extended for miles across the ancient landscape. If we could pile these flows one on top of the other, they would reach to thousands of feet. [See Wiki: "Staffa basalt flows." Accessed 2/8/19.]

The result of all this volcanic activity was what geologists now call the North Atlantic Volcanic Province (NAIP), a basaltic plain centered in Iceland. The NAIP is still active as the continuously erupting volcanoes on Iceland attest. [See Wiki: "North Atlantic Igneous Province." Accessed 12/2/18.]

SFA-2: *We Just Want to Go with the Flow*: Hot Lavas and Cool Basalts.

Like people looking to buy a new home, lava flows have strong preferences as to where they want to settle down and cool off. Nice flat surfaces free of obstacles, hills and/or pits are ideal. Unfortunately, the earth's surface is seldom flat and obstacle free. There are always rivers to cross, hills to flow over, dams to pile up behind, and valleys to fill. Lava just has to go with the flow and start cooling wherever it stops moving.

The ideal lava flow under ideal conditions would cool into basalt columns that have six regular and equal sides that would continue unaltered from top to bottom. Lava cools in much the same way that fudge, a spilled gallon of paint, or a big mud puddle dries: by drawing inward from its edges. When the strain of pulling towards a center becomes too much, cracks develop and a network of polygonal--many sided--"plates" forms across the surface.

SFA-2a: Looking down on a typical basalt column

(Note that the columns do not appear very hexagonal in cross section.) Looking at the picture above and at basalts you are walking over and among, observe the great variability many have columns with exactly six sides? What is the smallest number of sides you see forming any one column? What is the largest number? Look at any wall of columns, how many are distorted or irregular? How tall is the tallest of the columns? How short the shortest?

The variability in the height, width and number of sides of basalt columns is caused, in large part by:

(1) the nature of the surface over which the lava flowed or into which it intruded, (2) any post emplacement jostling or movement of the flow while it was cooling, and

(3) any resulting "competition" for cooling space within the flow itself.

SFA-2b: Side view of nearly perfect, "six- sided" basalt columns typical of the lowest section of the Staffa flow.

Another characteristic of cooling lava is that its columns develop at right angles to their cooling surfaces. If the surface is flat, the cooled basalt columns will be vertical. But, if the surface is, for example, bowl shaped, the lava will cool perpendicularly to all surfaces and smush itself together in the middle. If the surface is dome shaped, the lava will cool into a mound. You can see the problem: there is not enough room for nice vertical basalt columns to form within a concave surface and there is too much room for them to form them over a curved surface, so the columns jumble together.

Staffa is comprised almost entirely of basalts, a very common igneous rock. Yet it presents some very uncommon features, which make it a must-see for geologists. The first thing that makes the Staffa basalts unique is the order of its rock units. Most basalt "flows" fit a standard profile, presented below in 'stratigraphical' order with the oldest rock units on the bottom:

C. A top section of scoria (basalt with lots of holes) or rubbly, irregular columns,

B: A middle section of clear, distinct, regular columns, and

A. A messy, rubbly section at the bottom of the flow where the lava flowed across uneven surfaces and puddled up around obstacles.

The basalts on Staffa are not like this. Here at the south end of the island where the basalts are thickest and their cooling zones most distinguishable, you can see that the flow looks as follows:

3. A top section of small but generally regular columns,

2: A middle section of jumbled, disorderly, barely formed columns, and

1. A bottom section of tall, regular, well-formed columns.

This atypical order of the "sections" within the basalts indicates that the lava flow did not break out onto the surface of the earth but instead flowed into that sill preexisting and quite thick layer of soft sedimentary rocks. This, in turn, allowed the basalt to cool by growing its largest columns in the most protected area, the base of the sill.

SFA-2c: The "cooling phase contact" between the "well formed" columns and the "messed-up" columns.

SFA- 3: *Things Are Tuff All Over* : Igneous Rocks of the Air. Why is this flow on Staffa different from a typical flow? Because the lava did not flow out onto the earth's surface. Instead, it flowed either over or <u>within</u> one very thick layer of that light colored "sand"—actually volcanic *tuff*--you see at the base of the cliffs. The soft, yellowish colored surface on which the Staffa basalt rests looks like sand but is actually *tuff,* an igneous rock that forms when clouds of hot ash are ejected into the air by a volcanic eruption falls, cools rapidly, then fall back to earth. The rock formed when ash that is still so hot when it falls to earth that its ash particles fuse together is called a *welded tuff.*

There are a limited number of things that hot magma can do when it is being pushed out of a volcano: it can:

➢ Flow out across the surface, forming lava flows like those on Mull;
➢ Puddle up into a large molten mass;
➢ Be ejected as globs, bombs, and strings of hot lava that cool quickly when exposed to air; or
➢ Be pushed out toward the surface of the earth so forcefully that it explodes upon contact with the air and forms into shards of gas and ash.

SFA-3: Basalt columns resting on the thin layer of yellow volcanic tuff

Because tuff is softer and less resistant to weathering than basalt, it erodes much more readily than the basalt. You see this happening here: the softer tuff is eroding more quickly than the basalt and undercutting the columns that overlie it.

SFA-4. *"Through Caverns Measureless"*: Fingal's Cave

Fingal's Cave is named for Finn MacCool (aka: Fiann MacCumhaill), the legendary giant who lived in Ireland and the west coast of Scotland with his wife, Oona and their children. It was Finn and his family who, according to legend, shaped many of the geological and geographical features around the Inner Hebrides. You can see some of their best work at the Giant's Causeway in Ireland. Here in Scotland, Fingal's Cave and perhaps Fionnphort harbor are named after or attributed to him.

Staffa is narrower at its south end than in the middle. If you turn left as you get off the boat and keep walking, you will end up at Fingal's Cave. Although its entrance is unprepossessing and, this being Scotland, there is no signage, you will find it.

SFA-4: Inside Fingal's Cave

As you enter the cave, look up to see, from underneath, how the basalt columns have been undercut (weathered out) to form the cave. Weathering of rock is caused by chemical, biological, and/or mechanical agents. Here, you can see all of these operating in the same space in real time. These processes are:

1. <u>Mechanical weathering</u> is the physical process of breaking rocks into smaller and smaller pieces, is usually caused by external agents such as wind and water acting on the rocks. Causes of mechanical weathering include:

> ➢ Waves undercutting the rock columns and exploiting zones of weakness in the basalt, even to the extent of causing columns to "peel" off their "cliff" faces.
> ➢ Particles—sand, small stones, even shells—flung against the rock faces by the waves, causing small pits to develop on the surface of the basalt.
> ➢ Freeze-thaw and wet-dry cycles that cause expansion and contraction of the rocks. This sometimes causes columns to peel off the walls of the cave.

2. <u>Biomechanical weathering</u> is the breakup of rock due to biological or organic factors. The most obvious of tools of biomechanical weathering here are the long, somewhat creepy looking stringers hanging from the roof of the cave. (You can see them as white streaks in the photo.) These are the roots of plants that are growing down into the cavern from the ground above. Their growth and the freeze-thaw cycles they undergo, exploit the weakness of the joints between the basalt columns.

3. <u>Chemical and biochemical weathering</u> is the weakening of rocks caused by chemical interactions between the basalt and the water. Photosynthesis, for example, releases chemicals into the soil which are washed down into the cave by rains, while acid rain reacts with and dissolves the basalt.

The scientist in **you** is probably impatiently asking: "Ok, ok, but how does a cave sing?" There is, as you might expect, a very unromantic geological explanation: the cave is narrow and its walls, being made of eroded basalt columns, are uneven, causing the sounds of different pitches and durations. The softer, higher tinkling sounds of the water falling from different levels within the cave make different sounds than the sloshing of the water lapping against the sides of the cave. The deeper bass notes are caused by the air that had been compressed against the back wall of the cave by each swell being released as the wave retreats. Because the cave walls are uneven and the swells of the waves are not uniformly timed, incoming waves hit the rocks at the back of the Cave and each other at slightly different angles, thereby staggering the "booms" and "layering" the "notes." Or it's Finn and his family band serenading you. Your choice!

SFA-5. *"Chill, Dude! Don't Be in Such a Skerry!"*: The Herdsman and His Islets.

If you visit Staffa at low tide, you will see what look like broad bands of different, dull, pastel colors seemingly rubbed onto the rocks, cliffs and skerries (small islands) that are scattered around the island. Some skerries look as if someone—Finn, perhaps?—has put a lot of styling gel on them and swirled them into elaborate punk 'up-dos.' (Our favorite is the "top knot" on the Herdsman.)

Unfortunately for folklore, the reasons for the varied shapes and colors of the skerries around Staffa are scientific and remarkably complicated. For example, the size of a skerry is due both to how slowly its original lava cooled after it was deposited and if there was any later movement that affected the size and integrity of the cooling basalts. (Slow cooling and lack of jostling result in thicker more regular columns.) The "color" of the skerry is due to a combination of the skerry's orientation to the sun, the shape of the emplacement of the lava flow, the amount of water and sunlight the lichens receive, and the localized resistance to weathering of the basalt itself.

SFA-5a: The Herdsman

Photo by Jennie Rekers, The Netherlands

The color of the Herdsman "hair", for example, is determined by the sub-species of lichen that grows in each microenvironment. Specifically, because the top of the rock seldom gets completely submerged and, thus, gets wet only from wave action, the sub-species of lichen that is growing here is, appropriately enough, *splash lichen*. The following photo shows.

SFA-5b: Black gannets resting on the Herdsman "hair"

Thus, the different colors of the rocks here are not because Finn and his children have been coloring with their chalks, but because lichens of different colors exploit different micro-environments. And since Staffa has more than its fair share of microenvironments, it has more than its share of subspecies of lichen.

SFA-6: *'Fin'agling the Truth*: MacCool's "Giant" Web of Lies Exposed. (A brief, personal essay by Corky)

Fingal's Cave is known as the "musical cave" both because the basalt columns that form the cave look like organ pipes and because the Cave actually "sings." To my ear, there were three different sets of sounds: a throbbing, prolonged bass note; a shorter but deeper booming sound, and a rapid, complex tinkling.

When I was there, the man standing next to me began to sing. He had a rich baritone voice and it filled the Cave with sound that complemented the deep booms from the back of the cavern and blended with the softer swishing of water at our feet. By the luckiest of chances, my party had been joined by a professional opera singer who said he had wanted to hear what all the fuss was about. "He sang the tides into the Cave. It was magical!" (I swear I state this objectively, as a scientist.)

You may not be surprised to learn that Finn McCool himself had nothing to do with the naming of Fingal's Cave, even though it has helped keep his memory alive for almost two centuries. Finn's connection with the Cave was due to, what we today would call a <u>typo</u>, a simple error in transcription, like we each make every day.

The original Gaelic name for what is now Fingal's Cave was *An Uamh Bhin*, which translates as "the melodious cave." (Makes sense!) The problem arose when the famous composer Felix Mendelssohn visited the Cave in 1829. Like many of us, he was so enchanted by the "music" of the Cave and by the landscape of Scotland that he decided to write a symphonic piece in honor of his experiences here.

By 1832, he had completed the work, naming it, sensibly, **The Hebridean Overture.** A consummate showman, he decided to premier the work in London, where it would create the most "buzz." Posters were to be printed announcing the event!

Unfortunately, someone, probably a lowly, poorly paid, and now thankfully anonymous apprentice, was assigned to set the type for the posters. Not being extremely well educated in Gaelic (who in London was then or is now for that matter?) and probably rushed to get the posters printed, the poor apprentice set the type of the title of the symphony as "*An Uamh* **Bhin,**" the 'Cave of Music' as "*An Uamh* **Finn**" the 'Cave of Finn.' No one caught the error, the printer himself, if he proofread the poster, probably did not write Gaelic. So, the posters were printed with the error!

It was an understandable mistake. The words *Bhin* and *Finn* both look and sound alike. Even if someone had proofed the text, few in London, let alone a typesetter's apprentice or even the printer himself, were fluent enough in Gaelic to recognize it as an error. Everyone was rushing to get the posters printed and distributed; no one contacted Mendelssohn to check them.

When the good people of London saw the posters, they were delighted. They thought that Mendelssohn was acknowledging their ancient Gaelic cultural heritage, not complimenting the musical quality of a *cave*. Soon, all of Great Britain learned the myths of Finn the Giant, embraced all things Gaelic, and never looked back. It remains Fingal's Cave to this day.

As you return to the boat landing and depart, look around. Staffa is disappearing before your eyes. You can see the dark colored basalts being undercut by the rapid erosion of the softer tuff underneath them. Soon, in geological time at least, the island will collapse, section by section, and we will be left with a series of skerries where the music used to be.

END TRIP 1

Recommended Listening: Listen to Mendelssohn's Hebridean Overture and see wonderful pictures of the Highlands by entering "Hebridean Overture" in a search engine.

For More Information: *The Isle of Staffa* by Alastair de Watteville @ The Internet Guide to Scotland is excellent and goes into more detail than we can in this Guide. You will find other excellent books and resources at the shops around town.

> **Fun with Geology:** To visualize the ways that basalt columns can be affected by the surfaces over which they cool—but in extremely small scale--buy some of those log-shaped, chocolate candies sold at most every gas station and grocery store in the world. (We cannot use their trademarked name, but it rhymes with creatures you never want to watch a movie with--Footsie Trolls.)

Candy pretending to be basalt columns

Unwrap the candies and stick them together long side against long side. Vary the heights of the candies. You have made "cooled basalt columns" in miniature. Next, squeeze the candies together at the bottom, and look at what happens: the "tops" of the columns spread out. Then, invert your hand as you hold onto the candies, forming a trough. You are mimicking the ways that basalt lava cools as it flows over and around obstacles.

TRIP 2
"Mulling It Over"
A Guide to the Geology of
Six Road Accessible Sites on
Southern Mull
(MUL)

Sections 2-6 of the Guide are organized around specific "Stops"--places where, most of the time, you can park your car and learn about the geology you see from that location. This trip across southwest Mull begins at Fionnphort, pronounced as far as we can tell as *fin-a-port, and* ends at Duart Castle. Plan to spend at least 2-3 hours for this trip.

CONTENTS

Location, Caveats, Special Information, and Helpful Hints
MUL-1: *To Mull—To Think About Carefully:* Iona, Mull and Their Many Faults
MUL-2: *You Walk the Beach; I'll Comb Machair:* A Unique and Threatened Ecosystem
MUL-3: *Won't You Be Moine?:* When Bad Things Happen to Good Rocks
MUL-4: *...And Many More:* The Layer Cake Geology across Loch Scridain
MUL-5: *It's an Eruption, It's a Blow Out:* The Many Lives and Deaths of Mull's Supervolcanoes
MUL-6: *Finding Fault at Duart Castle*: The View from a Hill

CAVEATS, SPECIAL INFORMATION, and HELPFUL HINTS

This Section helps you understand some of the reasons why the Isle of Mull is a haven for geologists. We are sorry that we can only show you six of the thirty or so features that are essential to understanding the island's remarkable geology and hope you will return to learn more. And we realize that most of you have already driven from Craignure to Fionnphort and may be wondering why we have oriented this trip to take you from west to east instead of east to west. The reason: the geology is easier to understand going from west to east, and you are probably going back that way anyway.

One of the most important concepts in Geology is the idea of the **geological cross section,** aka "section," which is a presentation of the rock units in a specific area arrayed in their geo-time relationships to each other. (A geological section is a bit like a human genealogy chart if that chart showed not just name, sex, and birth and death years of the people, but their eye color, left or right handedness, height and weight.

> **Directions:** In Fionnphort, park anywhere you can find a place and walk around the town and harbor and along the beach. If the day is clear and you are able, climb above the harbor itself, either by climbing above the road near the jetty or following the path that goes along the beach and around the cemetery. Stop any where you have a good view of the harbor and Iona, the island west of the town. The view is amazing. But, it's more to it than that because the geology here is amazing. The Sound of Iona, the narrow body of water separating Mull and Iona may not look like much, but it hides amazing geological secrets.

MUL-1: *"To Mull—To Think About Carefully"*: Iona, Mull, and Their Many Faults

This Stop discusses the geological story of Iona, Mull, and Fionnphort.

Location: Fionnphort, Mull. [56.19.49 N, 6.24.12 W.]

09.09.2013 17:14

Split Rock and the Granites of Fionnphort Harbor, Mull

Discussion: We will begin with where we are. "Fionnphort" literally means "White Port." Since anyone in Fionnphort can see that the many rocks scattered around the port are pink, not white, we have to believe that the founders of the town meant something else than a reference to the rocks. We believe that the name was probably, originally, a reference to the to the Norse, who controlled Mull, the rest of the Inner and Outer Hebrides, and most of the west coast of the Highlands from 793 AD until about 1300 AD.

Unlike the original inhabitants of Scotland who have been described as a short, black haired people and called by historians the "Picts," the Norse were then, as they are today, tall and blond with pale complexions. Thus, the original name Fionnphort probably meant "Port of the White-haired Ones" and got shortened to "White Port." Or it could have meant the "Port of Finn MacCool," the local Giant. As far as we know, he could have been blond and fair skinned.

On any day other than the overcast morning when we took this picture, Fionnphort is the *cheeriest* harbor in Scotland! The "most colorful" is certainly Tobermory, the largest city on Mull, located on the northeastern shore of the island. It is colorful because of its brightly painted buildings. Fionnphort is cheerful because of the pinkish tinted rocks around the harbor. These rocks are the justly famous Ross of Mull granites

<u>Granites</u>. Fionnphort is built on the 'Ross of Mull granites,' the beautiful pink rocks you see all around you. They are considered some of the most beautiful granites in the world because of their distinctive colors and the uniformity of their crystals. Granites from Fionnphort were used in buildings and bridges around the world until the quarries closed in the 1950's.

Granite is an igneous rock that cools slowly enough that large crystals are able to form. The pink crystals you see are orthoclase; the whitish crystals are plagioclase, the grayish, translucent crystals are quartz, and the black flaky crystals are mica (biotite). Basalts, like those you saw on Staffa, are also *igneous rocks* but look different than granites because they cooled from a molten to a solid state more quickly because they were "deposited" in different environments--at or near the surface in the case of basalts versus deep within the earth's crust in the case of granites. Interestingly and somewhat counter intuitively, granites form the continental crusts, which can be up to 40 miles in thickness, while basalts make up the oceanic crust, which is approximately 4 miles in thickness. Imagine the force it took to lift these granites up to and above the surface of the earth.

Because they do not have bedding planes as do sedimentary rocks or columns like basalts, granites have few zones of weakness that can be exploited by weathering agents such as wind and water. Instead, granites weather by a process called *exfoliation*, the same process that our skin goes through when recovering from sunburn. *This is why all the rocks in the harbor are rounded*. Exfoliational weathering on a grand scale is responsible for many other famous geological features including Half Dome in Yosemite Park, the Black Hills of South Dakota, and Sugar Loaf in Rio de Janerio, Brazil.

<u>Thrust Faults.</u> Now look west across the Strait of Iona at the Isle of Iona forming the horizon. It seems pretty unassuming: the water is usually calm and, since Iona is less than a mile away, you can see the Iona Abbey as well as houses and pathways. But, as is so often the case, "looks can be deceiving." The water of the Strait of Iona hides an amazing geological event: the westward limit of the Moine thrust fault runs through this narrow strait, making Iona's rocks at least 1000 million years older than the oldest rocks on Mull. To put this in perspective, this is like your teenage son carrying your grandfather

around on his shoulders—something that is clearly not impossible but definitely not the normal order of things. And it is a clear indication that something amazing must have happened.

View of Split Rock in Fionnphort Harbor and the Isle of Iona
The Moine thrust runs just off the west shore of the Island as indicated by the arrow.

Question: So what was it? *Answer*: A thrust fault. A thrust fault is the geologists' term for an earth movement on such a massive scale that older rock units are pushed over and on top of younger rock units. The thrust fault you see here is called "the Moine thrust." It picked up and carried piles of sedimentary rocks from eastern Scotland and pushed them (*thrust*) over the top of older rocks in western Scotland. And that thrust stopped about just at what is now the east coast of Iona. We know this because many of the rocks that crop out along the eastern shore of Iona are *mylonites*. And mylonites are like press agents--telling you that a star has arrived. You will meet them again!

Close up of mylonites along Harbor Beach on Iona

But wait, there's more. Scotland itself is pieced together, like a quilt, from land carried here by six different major faults: the delightfully named "Iapetus Suture," the Southern Uplands Fault, the Highland Boundary Fault, the Great Glen Fault, the Moine Thrust Fault, and the Outer Islands Thrust. Two of these, the Great Glen Fault and the Moine Thrust bound Mull on the southeast and the west northwest respectively. (See Stop MUL-6.) There will not be a test.

Beaches. As you walk around Fionnphort harbor, think for a moment about the beaches you see here. Beaches are contradictions in terms: each beach is unique, yet all beaches are essentially the same.

There is a geological principle that explains this seeming contradiction—the principle of *uniformitarianism*--which, fortunately, does not mean that everyone has to wear those ugly, junior high school gym uniforms while studying geology. Rather, principle of uniformitarianism means that, in terms of geological processes, **the present is the key to the past**. Specifically, that the earth's *processes* have been the same through all time, so we can understand what happened on earth in the past by studying what is happening today. Scale and timing may be different in every case but the processes that affect the earth's lithosphere (rocks) are always the same.

We use the *principle of uniformitarianism* when we bake. For example, I expect that cake batter baked in the oven at a certain temperature for a certain number of minutes will rise and be delicious to eat whether I am following my grandmother's 100 year old recipe or using a recently purchased box of cake mix. And this will hold true whether the cake is chocolate or vanilla, whether the cake pans used are round or square, or whether I frost them or not. In other words, "when we learn how things are happening to and on the earth now, we can extrapolate to how they happened in the past."

> **Directions:** In Fionnphort, return to your car and head south out of town towards Fidden. There is a sign marking the road. Drive to Fidden Farms and park or follow the road south to other vantage points.

MUL-2: *You Walk the Beach; I'll Comb Machair:* A Unique and Threatened Ecosystem

This Stop discusses the evolution and future of machairs, an ecosystem that is at least a thousand years old. It is a system that has integrated human, biological and geological into a complex, interdependent network. And it is found only on the Atlantic/North Sea facing beaches of Scotland. Unfortunately, even though the Machair ecosystem evolved here in the Hebrides, it is disappearing into the "great ecosystems of history" in large part due to neglect.

Location: Fidden, Mull. [56.19.49 N, 6.24.12 W.]

Discussion: Fidden Farms is an actively farmed—rather than golf club managed—*machair ecosystem*, even though many people on Mull do not seem to know this. The word "machair" itself is Gaelic meaning "fertile plain." A machair is a very complex and integrated ecosystem found only on 'sea facing' beaches in Ireland, the Inner and Outer Hebrides, and Scotland. Miraculously, the machairs on Mull are surviving, even though no one seems to know about them. However, take away the modern buildings, the roads, and the motor vehicles and this area looks very much as it would have looked 500 or even 1000 years ago. (If you want to see a more robust machair, go to the west coast of Iona and walk inland from the beach.)

Machair near Fidden, Isle of Mull

Unlike most beaches in say the United States or Europe, a machair beach is composed of fragments of shells rather than rocks. And almost all of the shell fragments come from the shells of creatures that live in the Caribbean Sea and along the coasts of the Carolinas, Georgia and Florida. That's right. The Americas! "the photo in the next page" shows these white, calcareous sands at low tide.

Calcareous (White) Machair Sands near Fidden

Machairs are unique ecosystems because they have integrated human as well as natural and geological inputs into an interdependent whole. In other words, machairs evolved to require and reward both human and natural inputs. A typical machair has the following ecological zones--running inland from the beach:

- The drift line (high tide line) which is frequently covered by kelp strands,
- Dunes,
- Plains/grasslands,
- Salt marshes and lagoons,
- Heaths, fens and bogs, and
- Sea lochs and land-locked lochans (Say that five times really fast.)

Here's how this ecosystem worked in its heyday:

➤ Clams, mollusks, and the occasional crabs and lobsters died in the Atlantic Ocean and the Caribbean Sea and their shells float away and are carried by the currents to the coast of Scotland and Ireland.

➤ The shells are broken up into small pieces by wave action and by being smashed against rocks and obstacles.

➤ These shards of shells (aka sand) float are carried on the Atlantic Ocean currents until they reach and are deposited on the ocean facing beaches of Scotland and the Hebrides.

➤ High tides and prevailing winds push the mish mash of shells, sand, dead kelp strands, and other debris ashore, both creating and replenishing the beaches and dunes.

➤ Grasses and other plants grow on the dunes mix with the kelp strands trap the shell "sands" on the beaches.

➤ Rotting kelp fertilizes the machair sands, softens the impact of waves and protects beaches from erosion. It also provides breeding environments for sand flies and other insects, which, in turn, feed a wide variety of birds including starlings, plovers, wading birds, and gulls.

➤ Birds and their eggs feed humans and small animals such as foxes and, the newly reestablished martens.

➤ Cattle and sheep range freely over the machairs and trample the grasses which, in-turn, provide shelter for mice, birds, rabbits and foxes.

➤ Wild flowers growing among the grasses provide honey, the only sweet thing available to Europeans until the discovery sugar cane and sugar beets in the Americas.

➢ Machairs grasses lack significant nutrients, including calcium, that cattle and sheep need to reproduce successfully. These nutrients are found in grasses that grew only inland of the machairs. This meant that, in the autumn, cattle and sheep had to be driven inland from the coasts to graze on grasses that had possessed the missing nutrients that grew there. Of course, whole families went together. In addition to minding the animals, games were played, husbandry and home making tips were shared, and courtships ensured. It must have been like a clan gathering, family reunion, Highland games, and husbandry lessons all rolled into one!

Machairs are one of the few ecosystems in the world that succeeded in integrating human and natural inputs and outtakes. In other words, machairs not only meshed plant, animal, and human inputs, they required and promoted human interaction with the ecosystem.

Unfortunately, times have changed, and machair ecosystems are now being lost due to a wide range of factors including:

- The elimination of crofting as a viable lifestyle, due in no small part to the Highland Clearances.
- Fewer people actively living on and managing machair land.
- The under-grazing of the machairs by sheep and cattle. (Believe it or not.)
- The shift to "certified" seeds which increased yields but required fertilizers and herbicides which killed birds and small animals.
- Shift of management focus from sustainability to profitability.
- Increased tourism, and, with that:
- Locating golf courses on machairs and managing the land for golfing (and for big game hunting) rather than habitat integration and protection, and
- Building wind farms which destroy the machairs. Of wind farms, Malcolm Ryder says, "The Highlands are being humiliated by wind farm developers who insist they are saving the environment. They lie…" (Rider, p. 209.)

To sum up, machairs were, historically, a balanced ecological <u>and</u> social system that relied almost equally on earth, plant, animal and human inputs and outtakes. It "worked" for at least a thousand years. (There is some archaeological evidence that seems to date a rudimentary machair farming/grazing ecosystem to four thousand years ago.) Unfortunately, now, an ecosystem that had lasted hundreds of human and thousands of plant and animal generations is disappearing before our eyes. All of this makes Fidden Farms with its active management of its machair ecosystem nothing less than a miracle. [See *Machair* in Wiki.]

> **Directions:** Return to Fionnphort and drive toward Bunessan. About 5 miles from Fionnphort, as the road turns east to parallel the coast, look for and turn into a small parking lot that serves a small fishing pier. The rocks you are interested in crop out in the cliff face just west of and above the pier. This outcrop is located on private property so do not climb up to see it. There should be some small pieces of silver colored *float* scattered around the parking area for you to look at.)

Moine rocks turned to schists by contact with the Mull granite intrusion

MUL-3:*Won't You Be Moine?* When Bad Things Happen to Good Rocks

This Stop discusses a small outcrop of *schists*, a metamorphic rock made by subjecting shales and siltstones to intense heat and pressure. Look at the rocks in the hillside above and immediately west of the parking area but do not cross the barbed wire fencing to look at them closely. You can find small shards of silver-white rocks in the parking area.

Location: 56 19 08N; 6 14 42W.

Discussion: These rocks in this outcrop are *schists*, a metamorphic rock composed of visible, elongated minerals such as mica and graphite (pencil lead). Schists often exhibit the shiny, platy (flat) surfaces you see in these rocks. Metamorphic rocks are already existing rocks like shales and sandstones that were subjected to intense heat and pressure while buried deep within the earth which caused the original crystal lattices of the minerals to reorganize.

These schists were originally shales and mudstones that formed along ancient beaches. And everything was proceeding normally for a shallow depositional basin until the rock assemblage rolled over a hot spot in the earth's crust. Then magma rose up beneath them, upending them and metamorphosing them into schists.

> **Directions:** Leave the parking area and continue north east on the A849 to the south shore of Loch Scridain. You will be able to trace this feature across Loch Scridain for many miles so you can stop anywhere you can find pull outs. Look across the Loch.

MUL-4: ...*And Many More:* The "Layer Cake" Geology Across Loch Scridain

Location: Looking across Loch Scridain at the dozens of basalt flows making up the Ardmeanach plateau.

Discussion: This photo shows the record of the succession of lava flows that poured from the Mull supervolcano to form the "layer cake" geology" you see across the Loch. These flows are appropriately called flood basalts, and they are repeated on this side of the Loch but we are too close to them to see them.

**MUL-4: The "trap" landscape formed by successions
of basalt flows, seen across Loch Scridain**

Discussion: As you drive, note the dark rocks on both sides of the highway. These are basalts, like those on Staffa. These dark, vertical "lines" are called "columnar jointing." They form as molten lava cools into basalt.

The mountainsides across the Loch look as if Finn's wife Oona made Finn a gigantic layer cake to celebrate a birthday: the dark basalt flows comprising the layers of cake and the greenish slopes between the flows, the frosting. The much more prosaic truth is that this mountain is comprised of successions of cooled lava flows and the sediments that formed on them, repeated many times over the span of about 5 million years. Each of the escarpments you see is a single lava flow.

This is a terraced or *trap* erosion pattern, and it is characteristic of flood basalt landscapes. It forms because the basalts are harder and more resistant to weathering than the sediments deposited between them and, thus, stand out as cliffs between the more gently angled slopes made of talus, soil, and ash. As you no doubt guessed, the thicker the sediments between one flow and another, the longer the time that sediments had to accumulate on the cooling basalts.

Geologists call the basalts *flood basalts*, because the lava flows they cooled from travelled for miles across the land, the way flood waters inundate lowlands during a hurricane. But the extent of the lava flooding would put even the worst hurricane created floods to shame. During the Paleogene, 65-23 million years ago, flood basalts covered most of the Inner Hebrides including Staffa, Mull, and the Ardnamurchan Peninsula across from you, but also Skye, Morvern, Antrim, and Northern Ireland.

But it wasn't all lava all the time. There were both short and long periods with no volcanic activity during which soils developed and plant and animal life flourished, unaware they were living on borrowed time, going about their business, oblivious to past catastrophes and unmindful of the inevitability of new ones—a little like us.

> **Directions:** Continue driving east toward Craignure. Note your odometer reading. After approximately 3 miles, look for a small layby (pull off) along the South side of the road. Pull in and park. Adults should be able to get out of the vehicle, but young children should stay in the car because the footing is treacherous. Look for outcrops of very dark rocks and chunks of dark rock scattered across the surface and on the slopes around you.

MUL-5: *It's an Eruption, It's a Blow Out:* **The Many Lives and Deaths of Mull's Super-Volcanoes**

Location: 56.20.12N, 5.58.42W.

The view from the floor of the caldera of the first Mull supervolcano looking towards the volcanic mountains it created.

Discussion: Believe it or not, you are standing at the very bottom of the *caldera* of the oldest of three super-volcanoes on Mull. Even on a sunny day, it's gloomy. The dark rocks you see here were left after the volcano finally blew itself up. (Think of the dregs left at the bottom of a witch's cauldron.) This is the first of three volcanic centers on Mull. The others, Beinn Chaisgidle and Loch Ba, progress inland from here in an almost straight line trending NW-SE.

The reason for this alignment of the Mull volcanic centers is *plate tectonics*, the movement of the earth's plates across the earth. The "tectonic plate" on which Mull was riding ran over a "hot spot" where magma was rising up through the crust.

The hot spot did not move under Mull to create the string of volcanic centers. Rather, it remained in place and tectonic movements within the earth carried the Mull plate over the hot spot, creating the three different volcanic centers. That same hot spot, gave us the Giant's Causeway in Ireland. Iceland is over it now. This is what volcanoes look like after they have blown themselves up.

If you have visited Yellowstone National Park, USA, you have been inside another "supervolcano." However, there, the volcano is still active and its "bottom" is covered by Yellowstone Lake. Here the volcano has blown itself out and exposed its roots, the very dark rocks you see in the photo, for everyone to see.

Exactly what makes a volcano "super" is a matter of some disagreement among geologists, in part because the term "supervolcano" captured the public imagination before it was defined and accepted by geologists. So, geologically speaking, a "supervolcano" is that has had an eruption of magnitude 8 (on an 8 point "Volcanic Explosivity" scale).

A single volcano can start out as a shield volcano, then develop a cone, then blow itself apart as a super volcano as it taps different types of magma beneath the earth's crust. Our Mull volcano, for example, probably began with explosions that covered the landscape in ash. Then it erupted at least a dozen times, sending floods of viscous lava flowing across the land probably both as flows on the surface and intrusions into some of those ash layers, as we saw on Staffa. Then if built up a shield shaped crater around its central vents. Still later, it formed a cone shaped caldera. Finally, the whole complex blew itself apart, leaving behind little but the black, crystalline rocks spread around the huge, dark, empty bowl you are standing in. And then the volcano did it again—creating two more igneous centers to the northwest.

And, to add insult to injury, during the Ices Ages, the western part of this area was home to the Mull Ice Dome, which centered itself in these three valleys. (With friends like these…)

Look around you for horizontal grooves that look like those in the photo below. These are *terracettes* or "little terraces." The American West is rife with these features, and they have been the sources of a delightful controversy among some geologist friends.

Terracettes from hooved animals

Cattle, sheep, and deer are active, but seldom acknowledged, agents of erosion

In the mid'1980's geologists who saw these features while mapping the basalts in Washington State disagreed as to whether these features were caused by soil slump due to the steep slopes of the features or by the hooves of animals compressing the earth as they walked across the hillsides. When two different geologists, both friends taking different sides of the argument, saw cows side stepping along the hills and saw wet soil compacting under their hooves, the controversy was settled in favor of the animals!

Directions: Continue driving east toward Craignure. (As you climb out of the Mull caldera, note a series of small lakes on the south side of the highway (your right) near the top of the incline. These are paternoster or "Our Father" lakes, so named because they look like a short string of rosary beads. They form as glaciers retreat back up a slope and exist until they are silted in, which you can see happening in the lake closest to the road). Continue on the A849 up over the rim of the ancient Mull crater and along and past Loch Spelve. As the road starts to swing to the NE, look for signs on the right marking the road to Duart Castle. Turn there, drive to the Castle grounds, and park. Then walk to a high point on the grounds around the Castle and find a place where you can see bodies of water in every direction except behind you.

MUL-6: *Finding Fault at Duart Castle:* **The View from a Hill.** This stop discusses the Great Glen Fault and the "piecing" together of Scotland.

Location: The grounds of Duart Castle. Duart Castle was built in the 13th century and was the ancient seat of Clan MacLean. It was restored in the early 20th century. The body of water to your left is the Sound of Mull. Across from you is Loch Linnhe, which marks the southern end of the Great Glen fault and separates Mull from the Morvern Peninsula and the Scottish mainland. To your right is the Firth of Lorin. Across from you is the Isle of Lismore.

Discussion: Despite its reputation as "the land of plaids," Scotland is actually a **patchwork** country, pieced together from the remnants of other lands (called terranes) that were cast off from ancient super-continents and "stitched together" by faults. The Great Glen fault is one of the faults that have made the Scotland we have today. You will see another, the Moine thrust fault, in Sections 4-6.

Scotland has been "assembled" from pieces and parts of other lands and continents by a process that used to be called "continental drift" and is now called *plate tectonics*. This is the theory that the crust of the earth is made up of enormous "plates" that "float" across the surface of the earth like air mattresses on a swimming pool. These plates are driven together and pulled apart by convection currents within the earth.

Since the earth is not getting any bigger around, but surface land continues to grow through volcanism and sedimentary deposition, something has to give. And this usually involves one plate being pushed over another. This process is called *crustal shortening*, which sounds like we're making a pie crust. The opposing process is, as you might guess, called *crustal lengthening*. It generally occurs when massive amounts of lava flow out across the sea floor from vents or pile up as successions of lava flows, like those you have been driving through and can see across the Loch.

Just before the beginning of the age of the dinosaurs, 250 million years ago, most of the Earth's land was joined together in one enormous supercontinent, fittingly called **Pangea.** ("Pangea" is Greek for *all land*.) At this time, what we now call Scotland abutted what is now New England and eastern Quebec in one enormous continent. This supercontinent helps explain why the geology of Scotland has more in common with the geology of Newfoundland, Greenland and the eastern United States than it does with England and Wales.

Because there was only one continent, which stretched from the North to the South Pole, there was only one ocean. Geologists have named this "world ocean" **Panthalassa**, which means "all sea" in Greek. But it seems that continents, like people, have trouble with long term commitments-- and divorce is always an option. About 200-150 million years ago, Pangea started to drift over the active mantle plume that is now located beneath Iceland. As the land rode over the plume, it was stretched and cracked until Pangaea was pulled apart into the two land masses which we now call North America and Eurasia.

Sometimes the lava poured out of deep cracks in the earth's crust and flowed across the surface of the earth, forming the successions of flood basalts you drove through to get here. Other times the volcano erupted more violently sending plumes of ash into the air and showering the landscape with bombs of fiery lava. And they did this again and again over millions of years, forming vast lava plateaus that are thousands of feet thick and extend, collectively, over 700,000 square miles. You saw a small part of these flood basalts on Staffa and have driven through them on your way here.

As the plate continued to drift over the mantle plume, additional crater/caldera complexes like the one here on Mull traced an arc of volcanoes that stretched from Glen Coe north northwest to Skye. The North Atlantic mantle plume, which was responsible for all this, is still active today. It has formed the island we call Iceland!

END TRIP 2

Recommended Reading

Friend, Peter. "Area 6: Mull" in **Scotland, Looking at the Natural Landscapes.** Harper Collins, 2012. Friend's Fig. 121 has an excellent, multi-colored geological map of Mull that is easy to understand.

Jones, Rosalind. **Mull in the Making.** (Available in Bookshops in Fionnphort and Tobermory.)

Stephenson, David. **Mull and Iona: Landscape Fashioned by Geology.** This is a must have for anyone interested in the geology of this amazing island. The photographs, illustrations and maps are excellent. It is jointly published by Scottish Natural Heritage and the British Geological Survey. We found it in bookstores on Mull and in Ullapool.

> *Fun with Geology.* You and some children can have fun with the concept of plate tectonics by putting some air mattresses, toys, and floaties in the middle of a swimming pool. Station children at various locations around the edge of the pool and have them kick or skull the water as they please: sometime fast, sometimes slowly, sometimes stopping and starting again. Observe how the floaties respond. Some should jam together, others should override each other, and a few should break away and drift around alone. Exactly like the continents, except faster, wetter and much more fun!

TRIP 3:

Through Eternity to Time

A Guide to the Geology of Six Road Accessible Sites from Ullapool to Inchnadamph (UIN)

This trip begins at the Rock Route sign at the east end of Ullapool harbor and ends at the Inchnadamph Hotel.

CONTENTS

Caveats, Special Information, and Helpful Hints
UIN-1: *There's No Pool Like an Ullapool*: Welcome to the Highlands
UIN-2: *Having a Wild, Torridonian Affair:* The Precambrian at Ardmair
UIN-3: *Knoc, Knoc, Knockan on Heaven's Door*: Scotland's Premier GeoPark
UIN-4: *It's Good to Touch the Green, Green, Grass of…Elphin*: The Many Blessings of Sedimentary Rocks
UIN-5: *Small But Mighty*: The Loch Borralan Pluton at Ledmore Junction
UIN-6: "*…who played the foremost part*": Inchnadamph and the Memorial Peach and Horne

CAVEATS, SPECIAL INFORMATION, and HELPFUL HINTS

We try as much as possible **not** to replicate the Rock Route and GeoPark sites you will see as you drive along. However, there are some sites that are just too important for us not to include. (In other words, Corky would be committing geological malpractice if she didn't include them among the six sites.) However, if a particular site is not included on this Trip but is a GeoPark or Pebble Route stop, we hope you will stop at the marked pull offs and read that information as well.

Directions to First Stop/Cautions: Ullapool, which fittingly rhymes with "gull a pull," is a busy port, a tourist destination in its own right, and the starting point for this trip. This trip begins at the GeoPark sign at the east end of Shore Street.

UIN-1: *There's No Pool Like an Ullapool*: Welcome to the Highlands

Ullapool is the largest city in the Highlands and the launching pad for the four roadside "geo-trips" that will take you from here to the North Coast. So, this is a great place to introduce you to three of the key concepts in geology that we will be observing and discussing throughout the remaining trips presented. These are the understanding of *thrust faulting* and the twin theories of *crustal lengthening* and *crustal shortening*. (A tiny bit of giggling is permitted here.)

Location: 57.53.47N, 5.09.18W. NH 130940. This is Stop 1 on the GeoPark Rock Route. The GeoPark signboard is posted along Shore Street, about 12 feet from the junction of Shore Street and the A835. This is also the start of this road log. The photograph on the sign board was taken from this site looking northeast over Loch Broom. The white line shows the line of the thrust fault.

Discussion: We took the following photograph from the parking lot of the Royal Motel. Again a white line again demarks the fault. We think our photograph is clearer than the one on the sign board.

The "Line" of the Moine Thrust Fault at Ullapool

Because it is warmed by the Gulf Stream, Ullapool has a surprisingly temperate, climate given that its latitude is about the same as Churchill, Manitoba, Canada. It was well situated to its original purpose as a fishing village and now to its present role as the gateway to the Northwest Highlands.

The North Atlantic Current, also known as the Gulf Stream, rises in the Caribbean and flows north along the east coast of the United States, then swings northeast toward Iceland and the United Kingdom. It is this powerful current that warms the waters around Ullapool and keeps the harbor ice free in winter. (See: "The Gulf Stream and its Effects on Scotland," "North Atlantic Current" and "Gulf Stream" in Wiki.)

Ullapool is a "Thomas Telford Town," which means that it was planned and designed by the architect, city planner, and polymath Thomas Telford. Telford also built the roads that opened the Highlands to vehicular traffic and, thereby, to settlement and commerce. Before him, you travelled around by boat or walked. Exhibits and information about Telford are in the Ullapool Museum on West Argyle Street. www.ullapool.co.uk:attractions).

A thrust fault, like the one pictured above, pushes one giant slab of rocks over and on top of another slab of rocks, while both are buried deep within the earth. (Unlike people, the size of the earth does not change as it gets older, so if new crust is being made somewhere by, say, volcanoes spewing lava into the sea, then an "commensurate" amount of crust needs to be "lost" somewhere else. The means by which this "shortening" of the earth's crust is accomplished is *thrust faulting, t*he pushing of enormous slabs of rock over and on top of each other while both are deep within the earth's crust. You can see the now up-lifted results of this thrusting in the rocks across the Loch. The result of this process is crustal shortening. Crustal shortening needs to be balanced out by the making of new land somewhere else. The lava flows you saw on Mull and Staffa are examples of new land being made, i.e. crustal lengthening.

When Corky studied geology in college in the late Middle Ages, continents were, well, just continents, large, oddly shaped, fixed, and stable landmasses. When geologists began to pay more respect and scientific attention to the longstanding observations made by grade school children that the continents seemed to fit together like pieces of a jig saw puzzle, the *theory of plate tectonics* finally started to gain traction.

This theory proposes that the earth's land masses "float" on the earth's mantle, pushed and pulled by convection currents from deep within the earth. Sometimes these currents drag huge slabs of the earth's land down towards the mantle; other times they force enormous slabs of earth over each other as happened here. Geologists call the process of piling slabs of the earth on top of each other *crustal shortening*. The processes by which new land is made, usually through volcanic intrusions and eruptions, is called *crustal lengthening*. You saw evidence of crustal lengthening in the igneous intrusions at Fionnphort and the trap basalts along Loch Scridain. The Moine thrust, which you see indicated here by the white line, is evidence of crustal shortening.

Directions to Next Stop: This "stop" is actually a two parter because it shows you Torridonian rocks and then takes you to the nearby Ardmair beach. Drive north out of Ullapool on the A835. About 3.3 miles from Ullapool and just before the road curves to the right (east) towards Ardmair-on-the-Beach, the road passes between low lying outcrops of gray rocks. There is a small pull off on the west side of the road, marked by a dark green sign to "Chalets." Park, exit the car and climb above the pull off to get a good view of the area. You are standing on Torridonian rocks, and they form the hill west of the pull out. After you have looked at the rocks, drive around the bend and park at Ardmair beach.

UIN-2: *Having a Wild, Torridonian Affair*: The Precambrian at Ardmair

This Stop gets you up 'close and personal' with a very small and, unfortunately, 'not-terribly-typical outcrop of the Torridonian formation. In fact it is just a small section of a formation that is several thousand feet thick and makes up all but the tops of the highest peaks of the mountains west-and southwest of here. You will see much more representative outcrops around Loch Assynt on Trip 4.

Location: 57.53.47N, 5.09.18W. NH 130940.

Discussion: The grayish rocks you see around you are part of the *Applecross* **formation** of the *Torridonian* **group**. (A *formation* is a sequence of rocks that share characteristics such as type, constituent minerals, fossils, and/or depositional environments. A *group* is a set of related formations.) The sediments that eventually became these rocks were deposited in terrestrial (earth surface) environments (as opposed to marine environments). At around 1000 million years old, these among are the oldest **sedimentary** rocks in the British Isles. And, if you could look to the South towards Wester Ross, you would see that there is much more to the Torridonian than the small slice you see here. Unfortunately, you do not get to be "up close and personal" with much of the Torridonian on Trips 4, 5, and 6, so it is important that you see a small slice of it here.

Also, unfortunately, this outcrop is not very typical of the Torridonian overall, because here the rocks are grey and its sand grains are small and well sorted, while outcrops elsewhere are comprised of red brown to dark brown sandstones, dark mudstones, conglomerates and breccias. Some of those conglomerates are composed of poorly sorted, larger than a bread basket boulders of the Lewisian. (Mudstones are self explanatory. Conglomerates are rounded stones of different sizes and shapes, jumbled together. Breccias are comprised of sharply angled stones jumbled together.)

Differences in the rounding, size, and sorting of sedimentary rocks tells us a great deal about the environment in which they were deposited. Breccias, for example, must have been deposited close to their source rocks or the "corners" of their constituent rocks would have been knocked off. Conglomerates, unlike breccias, have to have been in an active enough environment for long enough that their angular surfaces became rounded

The sediments that formed these Torridonian rocks weathered from and were deposited on Lewisian gneisses. You will see them in Technicolor at the "Multicolored Rock Stop," (Trip 4, Stop 4). The Lewisian gneisses were themselves already thousands of millions of years old when they were being weathered to form the Torridonian.

Considering that they are 1600 to 600 million years old, the Torridonian rocks seem hardly to have been affected by the passage of time or by their long journey from 80 degrees south latitude to their present position 57-58 degrees north latitude. And, except for some folding and faulting in the Assynt region, they have suffered very little in the way of folding, faulting or metamorphism during their long time on, and travel across, the planet.

Taking all the evidence from the Torridonian rocks here and "reverse mapping" them back to when they were being deposited, we get a picture of this area as a very large, stable, terrestrial, (as opposed to oceanic) environment with hills and mountains made of Lewisian rocks, which weathered to form the Torridonian. It was probably much like the Canadian Shield today, except the then "Scotland" was located near the South Pole, not the North.

To frame the uniqueness of the Torridonian in contemporary terms, it is like a car that has made it through a thousand demolition derbies and only gotten a couple dents on its front fender and a little over-heating of its engine.

Contrast these rocks with the schists you saw at the small pier west of Bunessan on Mull (MUL-3). Those sediments, though younger than the Ardmair by millions of years, were so heavily metamorphosed by the Ross of Mull intrusion, that they were turned into schists. Proving that in geology as in real estate, it really is all about "location, location, location."

Now continue on to the parking area above Ardmair beach.

Coordinates: 57.55.36, 5.11.40. NH1198.

Discussion: Here on Ardmair Beach, even the *shingle* is interesting. ("Shingle" refers to the flat, layered stones that form the beach which have obviously been named for their resemblance to shingles overlying each other on a roof.) As you walk the beach and look along the shore line, you can see a variety of *sedimentary and depositional features* including:

- ✓ <u>Cross bedding</u> is the layering of sediments cross-wise to each other. It is indicative of currents washing sediments in different directions across a beach or sand bar.
- ✓ <u>Ripple marks</u> are wavy patterns formed by stream or wave currents flowing over sand or mud.
- ✓ <u>Mud cracks</u> are filled "cracks" in a mudstone or sandstone. They form when mud dries in a shallow pond or tidal flat making the cracks, and is then quickly reburied.

What you will almost certainly not find among the rocks of Ardmair Bay are fossils. Why? Because the only life forms living in Precambrian seas were *stromatolites*. Complex, multicellular life had not been "invented" when these rocks were being deposited.

<u>Stromatolites</u> are the fossilized form of "cyanobacteria," which is the fancy name for blue-green algae. Yes, that yucky stuff that grows in poorly-drained, kid's wading pools.

But, fortunately, like all bacteria, stromatolites grow. And the waste product of growth is oxygen. And oxygen, "given world enough and time," literally, made all the difference in the world. So no scoffing. The family tree of every life form that has ever lived or currently lives on earth--plant or animal---traces its lineage back to cyanobacteria just like these.

> **Directions to Next Stop/Cautions:** Continue on the A835 about 10 miles to the Knockan Crag turnoff on the right. It is well marked with a sign on the left side of the highway. Drive up to the parking lot and park. There are rest rooms in the parking area. Walk from the parking lot to the Interpretive Center.

You will probably want to walk some of the trails, so don't forget your walking stick and water. You should wear long pants, a long sleeved shirt, and sturdy shoes. Because it rains here (a lot), you will need a hat and rain gear. And, believe it or not, you want it to rain! Rain keeps away the swarms of midges that leap into full attack mode the minute the rain stops. So remember to douse yourself with bug repellent just in case the rain does stop. You'll stink, but you'll thank us afterward!

UIN-3: Knoc, Knoc, Knockan on Heaven's Door: Scotland's Premier GeoPark

Knockan Crag is not just one of the most significant geological sites in the Highlands; it is one of the most important in the world! But it takes quite a bit of time to look at and understand all the exhibits. Please don't rush through it.

Location: 58.02.6N, 5.4.17W.

Web Sites: www.knockan-crag.co.uk.

Discussion: Knockan Crag (also known as Knockan Cliffs) is managed by Scottish Natural Heritage. There are excellent maps and exhibits at the Interpretive Center, although not all may be "operational" all the time. They include:

1. The Cross Section Wall. A *cross section* is a vertical slice through the geology of an area so that rock units are presented in idealized "vertical" relationships to each

other. As you walk up the hill from the parking area, you will find a man-made "wall" showing the rocks of the Knockan area. It shows you what the rock units look like and what their vertical relationships are to each other if you could find them all in one location. Looking closely at the rocks of the Cross Section Wall will help you identify them when you see them during the rest of your travels.

2. <u>The Continental Drift Machine</u>. This is our favorite exhibit! When it's working, it shows Scotland's travels up the globe from very near the South Pole to near the North Pole and back to where it is now! Even when it is not working, just seeing its "tracks" is illustrative. Scotland is a well travelled land!

3. <u>The Thrust Fault Machine</u>. This exhibit shows in three dimensions how thrust faults "moved" blocs of strata over and on top of each other. It also shows how different thrusts can act in sequence, pushing different slabs of rock against already faulted-in sections.

4. <u>The Statues of Peach and Horne</u>. There are not many statutes that honor geologists. This is probably because the work, though hard and important, is usually not well known or well understood. The reason Peach and Horne deserve their statues here and the memorial on the hill outside of Inchnadamph is not because they spent thirteen summers mapping the area between here and Assynt, although that was hard enough. No, the reason they deserve these commemorations is what they did for the geology as a science! Their revolutionary contribution in a nutshell? They let their theories follow their field work, did not "reverse engineer" their field work to conform to prevailing theories, discovered, named, and described the thrust faulting as the mechanism by which older rocks can appear on top of younger ones.

5. <u>Peach and Horne's world famous **Geological Map of the Assynt.**</u> A copy is on display here. The maps we found several years ago on line seem to have been pulled, so this is the only place we know where you can see the map itself with all its complexity and detail. Be sure to take a photo. You can also see the map as Figure 6, on page 44, of Rider's excellent book, **Hutton's Arse**, which can still be found in bookstores with good science sections.

An excellent, simplified map of the geology of the greater Assynt area can be found under "Figures" in Robert Butler's **The Geological Structure of the North-West Highlands of Scotland—revisited** at "sp.lyellcollection.org."

Now you need to see the evidence of the thrust itself! Follow the marked path and climb up to the outcrop. Signs show you where to put your hands to "span" the thrust fault. The "Moine," the name of those very dark rocks you see at the contact here and in the following photo. The Moine is one of the thickest, most laterally extensive rock formations in Great Britain. It was formed in littoral, primordial swamps of what is now England and was carried here by those thrust faults you read about.

UIN-3: The dark black Moine rocks loom over the Cambrian sedimentary rocks along the road to Elphin

Moine rocks are found not only here, but also on Mull (Stop MUL-3). They were carried here on thrust faults, as you see here and in Ullapool and will see at other places throughout your trip through the Highlands. The Moine rocks are aptly named because the word "Moine" is derived from the Gaelic word for "peat bog," a clear reference to its dark black-brown color.

A Geological Thought Experiment: Imagine that you are Peach and Horne and have been assigned to analyze this contact between the dark and light colored rocks. At first, it seemed to be a clear, normal contact between two rocks units, the bottom one older than the upper one. Then you realize, by looking at the fossils, that rock units are upside down. The dark colored rocks are far older than the lighter colored rocks below them. How could older rocks get on top of younger rocks? There were, and still are, only three possible explanations:

(1) The rock units have been wrongly identified and the dark rocks are not older than light colored sedimentary rocks, or

(2) The ages of the rock units are wrong and the dark colored "Moine" rocks are not millions of years older than the lighter colored rocks, or

(3) Something happened that somehow put much older rock units on top of younger ones.

Which would you choose?

It's easy to state these three possibilities in an essay when we already know the answer, but Peach and Horne had to prove or disprove each of them by studying the rocks. It took them thirteen years of field research, sample testing, mapping, remapping, and, even though they were great friends, a few arguments. But, finally, the truth of the third, least possible explanation became unavoidable: a force within the earth itself HAD pushed thick blocks of older rocks up and over younger rock units.

They called the mechanism by which this happened: *thrust faulting*. It was a revolutionary concept, and it had been first, if tentatively, proposed by Charles Lapworth, a professor of Geology at Birmingham University. And his idea unhinged him because he thought the thrusts were happening in real time.

When Peach and Horne confirmed his idea, if not the timing, by placing the rocks in the Precambrian era but the thrust faults in the Ordovician around 470 million years ago. These discoveries eventually led to our modern theory of *plate tectonics,* which describes continents as resting on enormous "plates" of rock that travel across the globe. (An Exhibit at the Knockan Crag Visitor's Center shows Scotland's long trip from near the South Pole, up to near the North Pole, and now edging back south again.)

It would not be too much to say, that, with their discovery of thrust faulting, Peach and Horne permanently "rocked" the scientific world!

> Continue on the A835, about 1.5 miles to the pull off and overlook just beyond the Elphin Tea Room on the left side of the road. You will know it because the hillsides near the road are green.

UIN-4: *It's Good to Touch the Green, Green Grass of…Elphin?* The Many Blessings of Sedimentary Rocks

This section discusses the reasons why the area around Elphin looks so different from the most of the country side you have been driving through from Ullapool to here and, spoiler alert, will drive through on your way to Durness. The story boards in the parking area very helpful and will not be repeated here.

Location: 58.02.54 N, 5 1.53.

UIN-4: It's so easy being green...here.

Discussion: The GeoPark sign in the end of the parking lot identifies several sights you can see from here. These are:

(1) All around you, the amazing green color of the landscape which is due to the soft water retaining qualities of limestones.

(2) Across the small valley to your left are glacial troughs (gouges) cut into the Lewisian rocks by the glaciers, and, across the road. (The Lewisian/Durness contact runs in the valley floor.)

(3) An outcrop of Durness limestones. (Note the anticline, the humped structure, in the limestones.)

We will discuss the first of these in greater detail. Except in May and early June, the Highlands do not, by and large, sport many shades of green. In fact, it has been said that the Highlands put the "drab" in "olive drab." But around Elphin, the valley is awash in riotous shades of green the year round. The reason? Plants! Being sensible life forms, plants prefer to grow on softer, water-retaining, lime rich soils rather than on hard, impermeable, water shedding granites, gneisses, and quartzites. Thus, while it is true that plants have been on the earth for almost 700 million years, are found almost everywhere on earth, and have survived fires, floods, droughts, and diseases, given a choice, they prefer to grow in warm, moist environments that have soils rich in calcium carbonates. In other words, on the east side of this valley. The lovely green colors you see here may as well be waving a flag: **"Here we be limestones!"** (You will see similar greening of the landscape along the North Coast around Durness.)

> **Directions:** Continue to Ledmore Junction where the A835 meets the A837, about 3.3 miles from the layby at Elphin. There is an access road on the right (southeast) side of the road just before the junction. Be extremely careful when you pull off the highway and put on your flashers. There is a lot of traffic on this section of highway, but you do not need to get go far from your car to see the features described. Note that the photograph below shows road signs that are no longer here. We have more recent photos showing the junction without the signs, but the rocks show up better on this one.

UIN-5: *Small But Mighty:* The 'Loch Borralan' Pluton at Ledmore Junction

This stop introduces you to one of two, small igneous intrusions in the area and the surprising, even outsized, role they played not only in creating the geology of this area but in helping geologists understand the limits of plate tectonics.

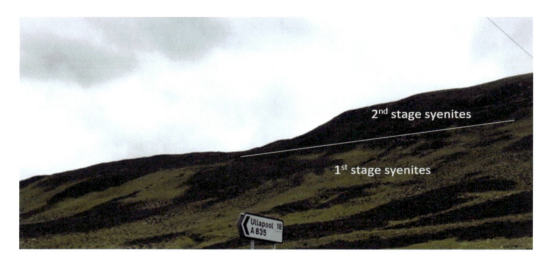

UIN-5: Mount Borralan from Ledmore Junction showing contact between the two intrusions

Location: 58.03.59N, 4.58.25W. NC 247 120. You are 17 miles from Ullapool.

Discussion: Mount Borralan is the somewhat euphemistically named "mountain" you see in front of you. Geologically speaking, it is a *pluton*, an intrusion of magma ("molten rock goo") that had forced its way into already existing rocks while all were buried deep in the earth. It has been uplifted to the surface where you see it now.

Molten rock goo" that flows out onto the surface of the earth is called *lava*. Molten rock goo that forms deep within the earth is called *magma*. The rocks that form the mountain are *syenites,* are igneous rocks like the granites of Mull in that they formed under the earth and "grew" clearly visible crystals. However, they lack the quartz and orthoclase minerals that characterize granites.

Look up at the mountain and find the gentle break in slope about one third of the way up the hill. It runs horizontally across the face of the mountain and is most noticeable at the far northern end of the mountain. (It is marked by a white line on the photograph.) This change in gradient marks the *contact* between **two** syenites of slightly different chemical compositions that formed the mountain.

To make syenites and granites, an intrusion of magma must cool slowly enough that visible crystals have time to grow. (Generally, the slower and longer the cooling of an igneous intrusion, the larger and better defined the crystals.)

That slight difference in the chemical composition of the magmas from which the syenites cooled has caused the two rock types to weather differently--with the more resistant to weathering "later stage syenites" forming the steeper slopes of the upper part of the hill.

The Loch Borralan pluton that emplaced these syenites was small, as plutons go, not much bigger than the mountain itself. (In contrast, all of Yellowstone Park sits atop just one pluton.) But, as plutons must do, it tapped the mantle as its source of magma. And that made all the difference in what happened next!

Put simply, **small though it was, the pluton moved the Moine thrust.**

In other words, the Moine thrust, with all the power of a converging tectonic plate behind it, was stopped and rerouted, into several smaller plates, by the Loch Borralan igneous intrusion. As Goodenough and Parsons state, "It is clear the pluton cuts across the thrust." In other words, the thrust did not move the pluton; the pluton moved the thrust. (This was a feat comparable to a bulldozer being diverted in its road leveling task by some kids who built a bonfire in its way! And there is evidence that the same thing happened around Loch Ailsh to the northeast. (See Chapters 10 and 11 in Goodenough and Parsons.)

So, in this area at least, the ending was a surprise: igneous intrusions, the earth's classic means of crustal lengthening, moved the thrusts and were more than a match for the compressive forces of crustal shortening. Or, to paraphrase the Spaniard in the movie **The Princess Bride**, "Never bet against a pluton, if thrusts are on the line."

> **Directions to Next Stop:** Turn left (north) at Ledmore Junction and proceed 6 miles on the A837 to the turn off to the Inchnadamph Hotel, which is sign posted. On your way here, you will see GeoPark signs for the turnoffs to the Bone Caves and the Stronchrubie Cliffs. Both are well worth visiting. At

the turn of to Inchnadamph, pull into the parking area on the right. This is where Peach and Horne stayed during their 13 field season trying to map the geology of this famous area. If you are travelling during tourist season, the Inchnadamph Hotel is a nice place to stay or just to stop to have a cuppa. The Memorial to Peach and Horne is located on the hill on the west (your left) as you drive north northwest towards Loch Assynt. You can see it on your left from the highway as you climb the hill toward Loch Assynt but there is no parking there. (!?!)

UIN-6: "...*who played the foremost part*: Inchnadamph and the Memorial to Peach and Horne [

The name "Inchnadamph" is to a geologist what "Cooperstown" is to a baseball player or "Nashville" to country music fans—it signifies a place where human experience has been profoundly altered and enriched.

Location: 58.08.05N, 4.58.38W. NC 252 216 and NC 248 222.

UIN-6a: Monument to Peach and Horne looking west

UIN-6b: Monument to Peach and Horne looking east

The Memorial to Peach and Horne can be seen on the hillside on the left as you drive from toward Loch Assynt, about 0.2 miles from the access road to the hotel. You can see it from the highway but, as of 2019, there is still no place to park. However, it is a very short walk. You should be safe if you pull as far off the road as possible and turn on your flashers.

Fittingly the monument is not enclosed so it commands a panoramic view of the entire Assynt region and serves as a reminder that Peach and Horne mapped in all kinds of weather.

Discussion: The Inchnadamph Hotel is the hotel where Benjamin Peach and John Horne stayed during the 13 summers they worked on the puzzle posed by older pre-Cambrian Moine overlying younger Cambrian rocks at Knockan Crag.

The Scottish Highlands have been source of great fascination and greater controversy for geologists since James Hutton founded the science in the mid 1700's in London. There are good reasons for this: Scotland is a small country with varied and complicated geology which is both like and very unlike the geology of England itself. In the early 19th century, geologists came to Scotland to study the geology, and almost all of them disagreed with each other when they did so. (Malcolm Rider's chapter "Deep Scar: The Moine Thrust" in **Hutton's Arse** is particularly insightful as to the reasons for and the effects of this controversy.)

It is important to know that prior to the work of Peach and Horne, geology had become a speculative science concerned with grand schemes and big ideas rather than a field science based on understanding the rocks where they were. Many people believed that the Earth was a certain way and looked to geology for proof they were right. Sometimes, as with Hutton at Siccar Point (see James Hutton in Wikipedia), they were right. Sometimes, as with Murchison who thought the Precambrian Moine was Silurian in age, they were wrong.

Eventually, the ongoing disputes about the geology of the Highlands became so acrimonious that the British Geological Survey realized they had to do something about it. So, they assigned to Benjamin Peach and John Horne, two staff geologists, the Herculean task of sorting out not just what rocks were where but how and why they got there.

Peach and Horne spent thirteen summers here in the Assynt area before publishing their field work. And make no mistake, this wasn't easy! Geology field work meant then what it means today: trudging up hills and down dales, being bitten by midges, digging pits, filling in pits, taking samples, being eaten by midges, retaking samples, measuring strike and dip, retaking strike and dip, tracing contacts across mountainsides and losing the contacts in landslides, being eaten by midges, walking over the same ground dozens of times, being eaten by midges—all the joys of geology field work.

They must have worn out their boots and gloves and overcoats and rock hammers, and their patience. And then they returned to London to spend their winters analyzing and probably arguing, and, finally, writing up the results of their work.

In 1907, they released their findings. The work and its geological maps of the area were definitive. (A copy is on display at the Knockan Visitor's Center and you can access a version sp.lyellcollection.org.) **The Geological Structure of the North-West Highlands of Scotland: A Memoir of the Geological Survey of Great Britain** settled all arguments. Peach and Horne introduced the concepts of thrust faulting, imbricate thrusts, dike swarms, and more. The geological map they produced was then, and remains today, one of the best examples of what geologists do when they map an area. And it is, dare we say it, "beautiful." It remains a testament to the "Art of Science." In his book **Hutton's Arse**, p. 42, Malcolm Rider describes this area as "soul finding country." He is not wrong. Everyone interested in geology should read this book.

Again, the only place we have found a copy of it that you can look at is at the Knockan Crag Visitors Center. Do not leave without taking a picture of the map!

END TRIP 3

Recommended Reading:

Rider, Malcolm. (2007) **Hutton's Arse: 3 billion years of extraordinary geology in Scotland's Northern Highlands**. Rider-French Consulting, Ltd. Rogart, Sutherland, IV28 3XL, Scotland,

TRIP 4
"Soul Finding Country"
A Guide to the Geology of
Six Road Accessible Sites Along
Loch Assynt
(LAS)

This trip begins at a layby near the middle of Loch Assynt (the second layby on the left from the junction of the A837 and A894) and ends back at that junction.

CONTENTS:

LAS-1: *"Islands in the Stream"*: Prosaic Reasons for Iconic Views

LAS-2: *Stumbling Across Deep Time*: The Lewisian-Torridonian Unconformity at Loch Assynt

LAS-3. *Criss Sauce, Applecross*: Torridonian Sedimentary Rocks

LAS-4: *No Truth in Advertising*: The 'Wanna Be' Basal Quartzites along Loach Assynt

LAS-5: *"Smoke If You Got 'Em."*: Pipe Rocks and the Sex in Cambrian Seas

LAS-6: *Twice as Bad!* : The Depositional Double Unconformity at Beinn Garbh

CAVEATS, SPECIAL INFORMATION, and HELPFUL HINTS.

The title of this section, "Soul Finding Country" is quoted from geologist Malcolm Rider's excellent book, **Hutton's Arse**, p. 42.

This Trip takes you through Scotland's most iconic landscape. You can see many of the features we discuss on cards, stamps, calendars, and t-shirts. And you don't need to be an artist to sense the special feel of the lonely islands of Loch Assynt. Everyone, even the most hardened geologist, feels the beauty and the loneliness.

Because, we want you to see the rock units in their correct stratigraphic sequence from oldest to youngest, we are sending you west to the "first" outcrop and then bringing you back "up section" from the Pre-Cambrian Lewisian gneisses to the Cambrian Pipe Rocks here at the junction. The north shore of Loch Assynt is Stop 8 on the Geopark Rock Route and Excursion 1 in Goodenough and Krabbendam's Guide.

> **Directions to First Stop:** Leave the monument to Peach and Horne and on the A837 2.5 miles north to its junction with the A894. This area is still called "Skaig Bridge" on some maps and by most locals, even though you cannot see the bridge as you drive over it.
>
> Other maps highlight the ruins of Ardveck Castle, ancient home of the Macleod's. It was built in 1590 and razed to the ground in 1672 by the Mackenzies, who built its neighbor, Calda House, in 1726. Calda House was destroyed by fire "of mysterious origin" in 1737. Neither has been rebuilt, probably the only sensible action taken in this long running feud.

Turn west onto the A837 and drive along the north shore of Loch Assynt, observing the islands.

LAS-1: *"Islands in the Stream"*: Prosaic Reasons for Iconic Views

This is one of the most famous landscapes in Scotland. There is something about the tall, graceful Scots Pines contrasting with the light colored rocks and the dark waters of Loch Assynt that speaks to the souls of many artists and photographers. And all Scots.

Location: 58.11.12N, 5.3.40W.

LAS-1: The famous Scots pines at Loch Assynt

Discussion: Saying "Assynt" to a geologist is like saying "Cooperstown" to a baseball player or "Nashville" to a country music fan. The words themselves evoke strong emotions. (Not that geologists are ever emotional!)

Look around you and note that the graceful Scots pines growing on the islands but not along the road or the hillsides here on the mainland. Why? The answer is, unfortunately, prosaic: sheep and deer eat any Scot's pine seedlings that start to grow on the mainland. But they can't swim! So they are not able to reach the islands to eat seedlings that sprout there. Thus, the trees survive only on the islands.

And the reason for their graceful, twisting shapes? Scots pine seeds fell into small cracks and crevices in the rocks where they are protected from birds and small mammals that might eat them. So they sprout and start to grow. But, they need sunlight and, like all seedlings, follow the sun across the sky as they grew. Unfortunately for them, and not for the plants on our window sills, the seedlings had to twist around as they "followed" the sun. They retained this 'twistedness' as they grew.

After taking "never enough" photographs of this iconic landscape, walk out toward the water line and look at your feet as you do so. You will see dark colored rocks running in straight "lines" across the peninsula. These are the justifiably famous Scourie dikes; they were intruded into the Lewisian rocks, about millions of years ago. You will meet them again in Section 5.

> **Directions:** If you are not already here, drive to and park at the second layby on the left. The entrance to the turnoff into a small parking area is just under 2 miles or 3 kilometers from the A837/A894 junction. Park, and walk across the highway to the small outcrop across the road (north).

LAS-2: *Stumbling Across Deep Time:* **The Lewisian/Torridonian Unconformity at Loch Assynt**

Location: 58.11.12N, 5.3.40W. OS Grid reference: NC 201261].

LAS-2: Corky standing in front of the Lewisian-Torridonian Contact

Discussion: These are not the "freshest" outcrops you will ever see. The rocks here have been through a lot and they show it. But they do have an important story to tell. Corky is standing in front of light colored, heavily weathered Lewisian rocks that are 3 billion years old. You can see the contact with the darker Torridonian rocks above her head.

Geologists call any gap or interruption in an expected series of rock units in a particular location an *unconformity*. Here, since the time gap between the emplacement of the gneisses and the deposition of the Torridonian is roughly 2 million years, we are safe in calling this an unconformity.

Gneiss is a metamorphic rock that forms when existing rocks are buried deeply within the earth where they are subjected to such intense heat and pressure that the crystal lattices of their constituent minerals change into different minerals and often reorganize into "bands" of like minerals. (You met intensely metamorphosed schists at MUL-2.)

> **Directions to Next Stop:** Return to your car and drive, slowly, back east along Loch Assynt, looking at the rocks you see along the north side of the road. The parking area is on the Loch side of the road, about 1 mile east from the previous stop.

LAS-3. *Criss Sauce, Applecross*: Torridonian Sedimentary Rocks

Location: NC 2194 2497.

Discussion: This outcrop is somewhat degraded and its features may be difficult to see. The darker colored rocks are sandstones and mudstones, more sedimentary rocks of the Torridonian formation. They may not look like much but they are the oldest sedimentary rocks preserved in the rock record in the British Isles. They are also among the oldest sedimentary rocks in the world.

LAS-3: Geology students studying an outcrop of the Applecross Formation.

If piled one on top of the other in one place, the Torridonian would be over 7 kilometers (over 4 miles) high. Here, you can see dark, thinly bedded rocks along the road. Malcolm Rider describes the contact between the crystalline Lewisian rocks and the Torridonian sedimentary rocks as follows:

> *…the Torridonian sediments are dated at 1.2 billion years… which is impressive enough. But the crystalline metamorphic rocks on which they rest come from very far back indeed and are nearly 3.0 billion years old, from when continents were first being created…The ancient Lewisian is now entirely crystalline, as befits its age. The covering Torridonian, although exceptionally old, is still fresh and, like Dorian Grey, shows no marks of passing time. (Rider, **Hutton's Arse**, 2005. p. 6.)*

Directions to Next Stop: Continue to drive east toward the junction with the A894. After about 1 mile there are several pullouts on the Loch side.

In summer, these may be filled with busses. Look for a place to park. If it's summer, look for white colored rocks and geology students.

LAS-4: *No Truth in Advertising*: The 'Wanna-Be' Basal Quartzites of the Assynt

Location: NC 2308 2453

LAS-4: Corky standing in front of the "Basal Quartzites."

Discussion: The north shore of Loch Assynt is the first place that you will see Cambrian age sedimentary rock formations of the Northwest Highlands in the field in their correct depositional order along the roadside.

As you drive back (east) towards the "Skaig Bridge" junction, you are driving, as geologists look at it, *up section* of the rocks. This means that you are going from the oldest rocks in the area, the Lewisian gneisses, through some outcrops of Torridonian rocks, to the youngest rocks in the area, the Basal Quartzites and the Pipe Rocks. The "Basal Quartzites" can look dull and unassuming on a cloudy day. But, in a burst of the late afternoon sun, they glow. Wow!

Unfortunately, these rocks are not really "quartzites" because there is little evidence of the recrystallization of the quartz grains required to make sandstone into quartzite. Instead they are quartz arenites--a particularly pure, well sorted, and well cemented sandstone but a sandstone nonetheless. However, these rocks have been called the "Basal Quartzites" by so many geologists for so long that we will continue the practice ourselves.

In other words, quartzites are metamorphic rocks that were once sandstones but which have been metamorphosed so that their constituent quartz grains have fused together, aka *metamorphosed*. These quartzites do not show this. So, although they rocks here are roughly 540 million years old and are among the oldest, unmetamorphosed sandstones on earth, their constituent quartz grains have not fused together, a requirement this rock to be properly called a "quartzite." Meaning, the Quartzite is just sandstone! A clean, white, extremely well sorted and extremely hard sandstone to be sure but still a sandstone.

But, these particular sandstones have been called "quartzites" for so long by so many people, including Peach and Horne, that the name has stuck and refuses to be dislodged by factual arguments to the contrary. So we too will continue to call them the "Basal Quartzites." And, fortunately, not everything about the name is wrong: these rocks definitely are at the **base** of something notable--the Cambrian era which saw the beginning of the evolution of multicellular life on the planet! And whether quartzites or extremely well sorted, almost metamorphosed sandstones, they are beautiful and Corky's favorite rocks in Scotland.

Directions: Return to your car and drive back to the intersection of the A837 and the A894. This area is still called "Skaig Bridge" on several maps, even though there is no longer any visible bridge. Park at the "pull offs" near Ardveck Castle and walk back to the intersection and down into the culvert on the east side of the road. Be very careful crossing the road, although once you do, the culvert is deep and wide enough for you to look at the rocks safely.

NOTE: Do not hammer on the rocks at this outcrop! If you want to study a rock close up, look around for pieces of rock that are lying on the ground at the base of the outcrop.

LAS-5: "Smoke If You Got 'Em": Pipe Rocks and Sex in Cambrian Seas

Location: NC 2349 2440. This is Stop 8 on the GeoPark Rock Route.

Discussion: The Pipe Rocks are delightfully and accurately named—they look like long, white, well-used pipes and bent cigarettes against a gray to reddish background. (I guess we know where Finn the Celtic giant snuck off for a smoke.) They can reach maximum lengths of up to 14 inches and diameters of an inch and a half. The red coloration is due to iron oxide staining of the matrix rock long after the animals died—a fortuitous accident which makes the pipes so much easier to see.

LAS-5a: The pipe rocks at Skaig Bridge junction showing side and top down views.

The pits you see are the tops of the burrows are the openings through which the animals fed. They have proven less resistant to weathering than tubes themselves which is why they appear indented when looked down on.

LAS-5a: Looking Down at the tops of the Pipe Rocks at Skaig Junction

Looking closely at the pipes, you can see that some of the worm burrows cut across many layers of the sandstones while others end after just a few layers. This means it is likely that:

✓ Since you don't need to hide in a burrow if you are safe on the surface, *Skolithos* dug their tubes for protection, which means that *they* had predators, probably trilobites. A *Skolithos*' predator probably used pincers to pluck *Skolithos* out of its pipe/burrow to eat it.

- ✓ The varying depths of the burrows shown in the rock indicate that *Skolithos* could survive and cope with changes to its environment. But we don't know if *Skolithos* was particularly long lived or if multiple generations of the same ancestors lived in the same tube.
- ✓ We don't see sand grains in the pipes themselves. This probably means that *Skolithos* could deal with minor (to us) environmental threats such as mud clogged tubes and irritating sand grains.
- ✓ *Skolithos* was one of the early active participants in the great sexual revolution of the—no, not the '60's! The 540 billions when sex was just being "invented. It was being "invented" by these extremely unlikely animals!

Unfortunately, as is ever the case in Paleontology, what we don't know about an organism like *Skolithos* is greater and much more interesting than what we think we do know. (Being worms with descendents still alive today, they are not the world's most studied animals.)   For example, we don't know:

? How did individual Skolithos or its gametes move from place to place to found new   colonies?

? What ate them, although trilobites seem to be a pretty good guess.

? What did they eat?-(Although cyanobacteria, aka blue green algae, is also a good guess.)

Cyanobacteria, aka blue green algae or pond scum, are the Earth's oldest living life forms. They formed massive colonies in the early oceans, which have been preserved as *stromatolites*. They were probably the bottom of the food chain for the emerging Cambrian animals.

Cyanobacteria have survived many environmental challenges over the billions of years of their existence, but they are essentially unchanged--the same today as they were those billions of years ago. And they have not changed-because they reproduce asexually, by simple cell division, from generation to generation, over billions of replications.

Cyanobacteria can thrive but they don't change or evolve. *Skolithos* had a different "business model." It reproduced sexually, which led to difference, adaptation, exploitation, and eventually extinction as environmental conditions changed faster than *Skolithos* could adapt. (Read more at: "Skolithos" at www.sjvgeology.org and Chapter 1 of Rider's book, **Hutton's Arse** (2007).

> **Directions to Next Stop:** Beinn Gharbh is the dark brown, flat topped mountain, 539 foot "mountain" south across Loch Assynt. (Not to be confused with Garbh Bheinn, the almost 3,000 foot mountain in Ardgour.) If the mountain is not blanketed in clouds, you can see two "breaks" in the slope of the mountain, one about a third of the way up and the other just down from the flattened top. On a sunny day, you can see that the topmost rocks are white to beige in color.

LAS-6: *Twice as Good!* : The Depositional Double Unconformity at Beinn Gharbh

Discussion: In geology, an *unconformity* occurs not when misbehaving children refuse to do something they're supposed to but when an expected sequence of rock units is interrupted and different rocks are emplaced over them. There are (1) *depositional*, (2) *structural*, and *(3) intrusive* unconformities. Beinn Gharbh is a depositional unconformity. [Note: The thrust fault you saw at Ullapool (Trip 3), the thrust fault at Knockan (Trip 1), and the "Double Unconformity" you will see ahead at Unapool (Trip 4) are tectonic unconformities. The pegmatite/Durness contact you will see at Sango Beach is an intrusive unconformity.]

LAS-6a: Beinn Gharbh Looking South over Loch Assynt

The mountainside of Beinn Gharbh shows us a *depositional double unconformity*, which means that, again reading "stratigraphically" from the bottom up:

(5) Basal Quartzites (Unit C) were deposited on that unconformity.
(4) There is another break in deposition (Unconformity 2),
(3) Rock Unit B, the Torridonian, was deposited over that unconformity,
(2) There was a break in the sequence of deposition of those rocks--(Unconformity 1),
(1) Rock Unit A, the Lewisian gneiss, was emplaced.

Thus the rubbly looking rocks at the base of the mountain near the Loch are our old friends the Lewisian gneisses. The dark, obviously horizontally bedded rocks above them are sedimentary rocks of the Torridonian. The contact represents a time gap of several billion years.

LAS-6b: Close up of Torridonian rocks

Now, looking up toward the top of the mountain, you can see a subtle steepening of the slope, and, on a clear day, glints of whiter rocks along the top of the mountain. This is not static electricity from Oona shaking out the bed sheets, but the sun glinting off the white, crystalline Basal Quartzites that you saw up close at LAS-4. Thus, this is unconformity #2. Since the quartzites are 500 million years old, this gap represents another 1.5 billion years.

But the thing most worth considering is the short distance between the quartzites cropping out atop Beinn Gharbh and the quartzites you saw at LAS-4. Over a surface distance of less than a mile, the Basal Quartzites have been displaced over 580 vertical feet. Nothing except faulting can accomplish so much displacement over such short distances!

TRIP 5

"...Between Rocks and Reason"
A Guide to the Geology of
Six Road Accessible Sites/Views
From Unapool to Keodale
(UNK)

This trip begins at the junction of the A837 and the A894 and ends at an unnamed overlook at the Keodale turnoff/rest area.

CONTENTS

Caveats, Special Information, and Helpful Hints.
UNK-1: *When Continents Collide:* The Structural Double Unconformity at Unapool
UNK-2: *Basalts Swarm Beach, Invasion Held at Bay!:* The Scourie Dikes
UNK-3: *That's Gneiss! That's What the People Say:* The Multicolored Rock Stop
UNK-4: *Knoc and Lochan Topography: Glacial Features in the Rhiconich Area*
UNK-5: *"As a Mark of Gratitude and Respect":* The Surveyor's Well
UNK-6: *Cat Scratch Fever:* Glacial Features Along the A838.

Caveats, Special Information, and Helpful Hints.

The title of this section is from Malcolm Rider's **Hutton's Arse.** Location: The e-article "51 Best Places to See Scotland's Geology" at scottishgeology.com is excellent and includes discussions of the geology of Laxford and Scourie Bay.

Directions to Next Stop: Return to your car at the Ardveck Castle/Skaig Bridge junction of the A837 and A894. Drive north toward Unapool, Kylesku and Kylestrome. approximately 5.4 miles from the Skaig Bridge junction As you descend the hill, watch for and pull into the large, well marked lay-by on the east side of the road.

UNK-1. *When Continents Collide*: The Double Unconformity at Unapool

Location: N 58.17.14, W 5.03.04. NC 240 295. Unapool. You are 5.4 miles from Skaig Bridge, aka the junction of the A894 and the A837. This is Stop 9 on the Geopark Rock Route. There are Exhibits at the Rock Shop and GeoPark Interpretive Panels in some of the pullouts which show the thrust planes and explain the movements of the faults much better than we can describe them here. So Corky is going to try to provide come context.

UNK-1: Glencoul: Where almost every break in slope is a thrust fault!

Discussion: Along with the iconic Scots pines on the islands along Loch Assynt (and the forthcoming "multicolored rock stop" near Laxford Bridge, this is one of the most famous, most photographed, and most geologically significant sights in the Highlands. It is amazing if you know nothing about the geology. If you know something about geology, it is both beautiful and amazing.

As discussed previously section, an *unconformity* is a significant break in a rock sequence where rocks of different ages lie one on top of the other, but out of the expected sequence. There are *depositional unconformities* like those Beinn Garbh (LAS-6) and *structural unconformities* like those here and at Knockan Crag (UIN-3), where the break in the rock sequence is caused by faulting.

A single break in a succession of rocks is likewise not unusual and occurs because deposition of a particular type of sedimentary rock was interrupted, there was erosion, and a new type of rock started being deposited later. Thus, an unconformity can be due to something as ordinary as, say, sand being covered by gravel as a river changes course or something as dramatic as a thrust fault pushing older rocks on top of younger ones. It is this latter type of unconformity that we see here and saw at Knockan.

Thrust faulting was the key to developing what we might call the "unified field theory" of geology. Just as physicists have long sought a "unified field theory of physics," (see WIKI: "theory of everything"), geologists have had their own holy grail--an explanation for what causes mountains to form and continents to move around the globe.

The answer is right in front of us, as it was for the early geologists, but it still hard to believe: compressive forces deep under the earth pushed (thrust) huge, vertical slabs of rock on top of each other and thereby shortened the earth's crust. Mylonites are the ball bearings of thrust faults.

> **Directions to Next Stop:** Drive across the "new" bridge at Kylesku which has been described as the most beautiful bridge in the Highlands, except, Like Skaig Bridge, you cannot see it as you drive over it.

> **Stop at the Rock Stop Café and Exhibition Center i**f you have geological questions, need a closer look at rock samples and maps, want to buy a

Geopark shirt, or just need a cuppa! It is signposted along the highway and features excellent samples of the rocks you have been reading about and seeing at a distance. as well as good geo-videos played on continuous loop. (Google: Rock Stop Café Unapool.)

After visiting the Rock Stop, continue on the A894 about 11 miles to Scourie. The parking area for the Cemetery is on the left just as you enter the village. It is sign-posted. Park, then follow any of the paths around the cemetery to the dark rocks cropping out along and above the shore. Also, look across the small bay at the vertical rocks cropping out along the shore.

UNK-2. *Basalts Swarm Beach, Invasion Held at Bay!*: The Scourie Dikes

Location: NC 148 448. Southwest shore of Scourie Bay, Scourie. You can see the dikes looking like the vertical intrusions they are in the outcrop across the bay.

Web Sites: www.earth.ox.ac.uk.

UNK-2: The famous, black Scourie Dikes with their usual colorful coating of Geology students

Discussion: A *dike* is any rock unit that cuts across the rock unit it is intruding into. A *sill* is any rock unit that runs parallel to the rock unit it intrudes. A dike and a sill are always younger than the rock unit they intrude.

The dark black Scourie dikes here are composed of now-metamorphosed diorite. They were intruded into the light gray colored Lewisian gneisses as the ancient Lewisian continent was being pulled apart, and lava was being pushed up into the developing cracks.

This intrusion of the basalts/diorites occurred over a period of 400 million years, ending two thousand million years ago. As you see, they are not showing their age much! And that is because, only 15 miles as the crow flies from Glen Coul, they have not been subjected to as much tectonic stress.

There are so many dikes in the Scourie-Badcall area (Corky has counted over 70 on maps) that geologists coined the term *dike swarm* to describe them—undoubtedly with all connotations of aggregations of angry bees and wasps intended!

These dikes and their relationships to the Lewisian basement rocks are useful in illustrating the concepts of *crustal lengthening* and *crustal shortening*. (This does not refer to Oona's attempt to bake a pie for Finn!) It seems deceptively simple: crustal lengthening adds new land to the crust; crustal shortening reduces it. Igneous intrusions (MUL-1) and lava flows (MUL-3) are the most common ways that the earth's crust is added to or "lengthened. Thrust faulting is the most common way the earth's crust is shortened. You saw both these forces acting simultaneously at Mount Borralan (UIN-5). You will see more evidence of both crustal lengthening and crustal shortening acting on rocks in the same area at Sango Bay in Durness.

> **Directions to Next Stop:** Return to your car and continue northeast on the A894 to Laxford Bridge and the junction with the A838, about 10 miles. The outcrops run for over a mile. We suggest you drive the length of the whole outcrop so you get a sense of how extensive it is. Then double back to find a place to park. Because this is one of the most famous geological sites

in the world, Scotland's roads department has actually provided laybys where you can park, get out of your car, and walk along the outcrop.

But you still need to be cautious. There is lots of traffic, and drivers either do not slow down or are themselves so interested in the rocks that they drive carelessly! Therefore, everyone should wear their hi-viz safety vests and take extra care crossing the highway or walking along the outcrops.

Plan to spend at least half an hour here.

Finally, do not hammer on the rocks. There should be enough "float" lying in the ditches and along the roadside for you to take a small piece home. (Not to mention that you are likely to more break your hammer than obtain a sample.)

UNK-3. *That's Gneiss! That's What the People Say:* **The Multicolored Rock Stop**

This is Stop 11 on the GeoPark Rock Route and the third of the three most famous geological sites in Scotland. The other two are the Moine thrust at Knockan Crag (UIN-3), and the thrust faults at Unapool (UNK-2, above). Unfortunately for the Scots highway engineers, and fortunately for us, the soft Torridonian and Cambrian-Ordovician sediments now lie to the south of us, so they had little choice but to build their roads on the Lewisian gneisses! (Although why they blasted through the rocks here instead of putting the road on top of them, as they did at Rhiconich, I have no idea. But I am eternally grateful. Seeing the gneisses in "cross section" is seeing one of the wonders of the geological world!)

The Lewisian gneiss is around 3.5 billion years old. It has been residing here on the surface of the planet for over 1 billion years. During that time, it has had every environmental force thrown at it—lava flows, desert sands, earthquakes, and many glaciers—you name it. Yet it looks pretty much the same as it did when it was first uplifted out of the depths of the earth and brought to the surface. We could all aspire to such steadfastness!

Location: 58.24.7N, 5.0.42W. NC 233 486. This is Stop 11 on the GeoPark Rock Route.

Cautions: There is a lot to see here and many people trying to see it all at once! So you need to be watchful at all times! Here, as at another popular geological site, Old Faithful Geyser at Yellowstone Park, people are often careless about their own safety especially when in pursuit of the perfect photo. So **you** have to look for them! They will not be looking out for you.

Finally, do not climb on the outcrop! It is dangerous. Gneiss, like granite, exfoliates, so it can be slippery and you can fall even when it isn't wet.

UNK-3a: Multigenerational banding in the gneiss

Discussion: Although the Lewisian gneiss formed the islands along the north shore of Loch Assynt and the rocks into which the Scourie dikes intruded, those were not the best outcrops, so we have waited until now to make formal introductions.

Gneiss is the name given to banded, metamorphic rocks. Pronounced "nice"—which it certainly is—gneiss is a rock whose original constituent minerals have been recrystallized and reorganized into "bands" of similar minerals and similar colors.

UNK-3b: Saltaire (cross pattern) in the gneiss

See if you can find 3 saltaires

All gneisses are interesting, but the Lewisian is especially so because the banding repeats in thin section, in hand specimen, across an outcrop, and across the entire area. To see this, pick up a piece of the gneiss from beside the road or the base of a cliff. Look at it, then step back so you can see the whole outcrop. The banding is the result of mineral segregation into light layers of muscovite and quartz and dark bands of hornblende and biotite. It has nothing to do with any layering in the original rock. [See Friend, **Scotland,** p. 374, and go to Google Earth and enter "Rispond, Scotland" for an amazing aerial view of the Lewisian here.]

Gneiss does share one important characteristic with granites, like those you met on Mull—exfoliational weathering. This means that only thin layers of minerals weather off the outcrop making the rocks appear rounded or humped. In the following photo, you are looking up the "nose" of a rock face suffering from exfoliational weathering.

UNK-3c: Exfoliational weathering in action.

Here's a list of features to look for as you walk along the outcrop from south to north, presented in chronological order:

- ➢ *Complex cross cutting relationships*. The Lewisian gneiss has been so mushed, stretched, and cross cut by intrusions that it is possible to "see" many common place objects in the rocks. The most famous of these is the Saltaire (St. Andrew's cross).
- ➢ *Multi-scale banding*. Not all gneisses do this: repeat their banding across a rock face and in hand specimen as the Lewisian gneisses does. In fact, as befits the oldest rocks in the world, the Lewisian repeats its banding over all scales: millimeters, meters, and kilometers.
- ➢ *Dark black rocks* that were once the Scourie dikes cut across the gneiss as do veins of quartz.
- ➢ *Boudinage* (sausage-like structures). "Boudin" means sausage in French. At the south end of the outcrop, you can see pink granitic intrusions within the gneiss. (They look a little like gigantic pink sausages, bulging in the in the middle and pinched off at the ends.) Boudinage structures are created when compressive forces within the earth squeeze semi-solid rock goo together. (You could produce the same effect

by putting big globs of three different colored cake frosting in a plastic bag, sealing the bag, and kneading it for a few seconds.)

➤ Large oddly shaped blobs of pink granite that were pushed into the gneisses the same way you might impatiently squeeze together two bags of different colored frosting before frosting a cake. They have been dated at around 2 billion years and are evidence of another period of the lengthening of the Lewisian crust, this time while the Lewisian was deeply buried within the earth.

➤ The seeming "dip" (slanting) of the gneisses from upper left to lower right (NW-SE) across the outcrop was caused by uplift and "shearing" of the ancient Lewisian rocks as the two terranes collided – a clear response to crustal shortening. The Lewisian is comprised of nine different terranes or blocs of ancient crust. You only see two here, the Assynt and the Rhiconich terranes.

➤ Large dark black chunks of the Scourie basalts cut through and across the gneiss. The effect of the intrusion of the Scourie dikes was to "lengthen" the earth's crust. They are between 2.4 billion years old.

Precambrian rocks such as these form the cores of all the continents, except Antarctica, where we may not have found them yet. As Malcolm Rider writes:

All the continents are like this…an ancient heart wrapped in layers of younger and younger mountain belts…When we touch the Lewisian Gneiss, we are touching the heart of a young continent, a rock reminder of our planet's beginnings. [Rider, p. 187.]

Directions to Next Site: Rhiconich is located at the junction of the A838 and B801 about 8 miles from Laxford Bridge. This is Stop 12 on the GeoPark Rock Route. There are several small turnouts along the road, but you can see most features as you drive along.

UNK-4: *Knoc and Lochan Topography*: Glacial Features in the Rhiconich Area

Location: N 58.21.01; W5.09.35. NC 246503.

Discussion: Rhiconich is a small hamlet at the head of Loch Inchard, and one of our favorite Gaelic place names. In this one small area, Lewisian gneisses do double duty as both the oldest (the bedrock) and the youngest (the glacial erratics) rocks in the area. Sweet!

Geologists have a term for the unique and characteristic Lewisian landscape you are driving through. It is called **knoc and lochan** (low hills/small lakes) **topography.**

UNK-4a: Knoc and Lochan Topography

Its signature features include:

- <u>Knocs</u> are the small, low lying, knobby "hills" you see everywhere. They formed from the differential erosion by the ice during the Pleistocene and are noted for lacking drainage.
- <u>Lochans</u> are the small, isolated lakes and ponds that are interspersed among the knocs. Lochans formed when glacial ice carved shallow depressions in the gneiss bedrock. They fill with water from rain or snow melt but are not connected to each other. A lochan can be any shape, size or depth. Some are large and

show little or no vegetation growing in or around them. Others lochans are shallower and swampy with flowers and plants growing in them. Still others are almost choked with weeds and algae.

UNK-4b: Lochan near rhiconich

- <u>Moraines</u> are the rock debris that falls out of a glacier as the ice melts. There are terminal and lateral moraines. *Terminal moraines* are at the ends of glaciers and retreat up slope as the glacier melts. *Lateral moraines* are debris fields that run parallel with the flow of the glacier. Terminal moraines often leave a series of *paternoster lakes* as they melt up slope. (You saw paternoster lakes along the roadside as you drove out of the caldera on Mull.)
- <u>Erratics.</u> The split rock in Mull Harbor is technically an erratic even if its source outcrop was the nearby Mull granites themselves. You can see others scattered around the hillsides here near Rhiconich and above Ceannebienne beach east of Durness.
- <u>Glacial erratics</u> are the large boulders you see scattered across the slopes. They are large rocks that were torn from their outcrops by glaciers, carried along by

them often for miles, and then unceremoniously dumped wherever they were when the ice melted.

- <u>Rock Scour</u>. Occasionally you will see piles of small rocks, often at the southeast ends of lochans. This is rock scour, the sandpaper of glaciers. (It's, not the ice that causes glaciers to erode rock but the rocks the glacier carries within it.) Rock scour It is dumped out of glaciers as they melt. But after the ice melts, there may be too little water from rain and snow to wash the piles away.
- <u>Knobs and Notches</u>. Rocks, especially rocks as hard as the Lewisian gneiss, do not weather easily or uniformly, even when the abrading force is glacial scour. There are always bumps and pits in the surface. The Scots have their own names for these irregularities: bumps are *knobs* and hollows are *notches*.
- <u>Exfoliation</u>. Exfoliation means sloughing or peeling off in layers. It is characteristic of the way that rocks like these erratics weather. Our skin does the same thing when it's sunburned. You saw exfoliation of the gneisses at Laxford.
- <u>Erratics</u>. Erratics are "displaced" rocks that have been transported by glaciers from their original areas to where they are "out of place" and, usually, do not match their new surroundings. The split rock in the Fionnphort Harbor on Mull is an erratic.
- <u>Flowers</u>. Some beautiful flowers grow in the lochans. Unfortunately, as the lochan fills up with silt and dead plants, the plants are get crowded out and the lochan dies. Fortunately, new lochans form all the time as rock falls create temporary dams among the rocks.
- <u>Bull Rush and Heather Scrubland</u>. If it's hard to erode the Lewisian when you are a good sized glacier; it is very, very difficult if you are just ordinary rain and snow—if such highland weather can ever be said to be ordinary. Only plants known for their hardiness—the bull rushes, heather, and the prickly yellow gorse—grow prolifically here. (The Great Bull Rush is the plant badge of Clan MacKay and the beautiful heather is the symbolic plant of Scotland. We could not find any Clan, county, or country that has so honored the yellow, prickly gorse.) (See Google maps and Friend, figs. 265, 266, and 2676, pp. 374-375.)

Directions to Next Stop: The Surveyor's Well is located on the A838, 15 miles from Rhiconich immediately after the curve in the road as it rounds the upper slopes of Mount Farrmheall. Do not stop! There is no turnout or parking place, so we will show you pictures and tell you about it.

UNK-5: "As a Mark of Gratitude and Respect": The Surveyor's Well.

Location: 58.28.37N, 4.53.6W.

Discussion: The Surveyor's Well is interesting because it is not immediately clear why it has been built here, so high above the valley floor. It is certainly not the most convenient location from which to get water—especially if you live in the valley! And there is no place to park!

UNK-5: The Surveyor's Well

So why is it here? There are two answers. One is sociological: it was an early "rest stop with water" for horse pulled wagons and coaches that had climbed a steep grade to get here. They had to have been thirsty! The other answer is geological: A small lens of Cambrian sedimentary rocks (sandstones and dolomites) has been faulted in here by those thrust faults we keep talking about. And those rocks "hold" rather than shed the runoff and snow melt. Yet another reason to be grateful for the vagaries of thrust faults!

But, as important as what the Well tells us about the geology of the area is the opportunity it gives us to think about the **roads**, specifically the roads you've been driving on and their role in the history of the Highlands. Before the mid-late 1800's, most people who lived here in northern Scotland were small crofters who got about by boat or by walking. Access to the interior of the country was difficult, time consuming, and expensive. And it wasn't all that necessary. Most people lived along the coasts, and most trade was with the people of Scandinavian countries (who were collectively called "the Norse") which were far more accessible than London.

By the late 1800's, the British government realized that they needed to open up the interior of the Northern Highlands to commerce and embarked on a roads building program to link the North Coast of Scotland to England. But building a road across terrain as difficult as the Highlands required several things: a stable enough government to carry out such a long range project (in other words, enough bureaucrats), enough money to fund the project until increased revenue from trade and taxes could begin to pay back the investment, the technology to build the roads themselves, ready access to road building materials, and, most importantly, a way of determining exactly where to put the road itself. This last required surveyors, those unsung heroes of any large scale, public works project.

When people put up plaques to honor those who built roads and bridges, a rare enough occurrence, it is usually to honor a mayor or governor who was instrumental in getting the project approved or funded. It is seldom that the project's worker bees are recognized, but not completely unheard of. But, here, at this remarkable well, we find the opposite: a surveyor who erected a plaque to honor the people who sheltered, fed, and encouraged HIM so he could do his work. It reads:

1883 As a Mark of Gratitude and Respect to the Inhabitants of Durness and Edrachilles for their Hospitality while projecting this road. This inscription is placed over this well by their humble servant Peter Lawson, Surveyor.

Directions to Next Stop: Continue north towards Durness. At 14.5 miles from Rhiconich, there is a small turnout on your right (east) as you round the curve. Park there or continue on to the Keodale turnoff about .2 miles ahead. Look east across the road at the slopes across from you.

UNK-6: *"Cat Scratch Fever"*: **Glacial Features Along The A838.** (With apologies to Ted Nugent.)

Location: View points and turnoffs along the A838.

Discussion: The side of the mountain looks like the back of a couch that has been clawed by a very large, very angry cat. As you might guess, these "scratches" were not made by Finn and Oona's angry pet tiger, as delightful as that image may be. Rather, the "scratches" are streams that have cut back into the lateral moraine that forms the mountain opposite you.

UNK-6: Cat Scratch Fever: Deeply Incised Lateral Moraines

Moraines are piles—sometimes, like here, miles of piles—of boulders, stones, pebbles, tree stumps and dirt left behind as glaciers melt and dump their loads of rocks, trees, sands and silts.   There are two basic types of moraines: *lateral and terminal moraines.* Lateral moraines are deposited along the sides of glaciers and they hang in valleys for thousands of years. Terminal moraines are always, duh, at the end of the glacier. They are created as a melting glacier retreats up its valley. Many melting glaciers leave a series of moraines behind as they retreat up slope. The retreating glaciers often form paternoster lakes as we saw on Mull. (From an aerial view, paternoster lakes look like (misshapen) beads on a Rosary.

The glacial features you see in this area look fresh because they are. Glaciologists studying features such as these all over Europe and have revised the dates for this most recent continental glaciation forward from hundreds of thousands of years ago to just 14,500 to 13,500 years ago. And they estimate that the ice sheet here in Scotland may have melted in less than 50 years. (Corky thinks there is evidence that the ice melted off the Highlands in less than a decade.)

In any case, it doesn't matter. The end of the "Little" Ice Age was sudden and its effects were profound. The floods resulting from the quick melting of glacial ice made and unmade cultures and civilization as well land forms and environments. And we are still feeling its effects.

END TRIP 5

TRIP 6

The More Things Change, The More They *Change*.
A Guide to the Geology of Six Road Accessible Sites from Kyle of Durness to Smoo Cave
KDC

CONTENTS

Caveats, Special Information and Helpful Hints
KDC-1: *'It's Not So Easy Being Green'*: The Kyle of Durness
KDC-2: *Mylonites, You've Got the Cutest Little Mylonites!* The Metamorphic Rocks of Balnakiel Bay
KDC-3: *He Been Havin' Some Far Travelin'*: The Old Man in the Outcrop
KDC-4: *And You Thought You'd Seen the Last of Them:* The "Basal" Quartzites Return
KDC-5: *Are There Any Schmoos Left At Smoo Cave?*: A Triple Treat Cave
KDC-6: *Play It Again, Finn*: Piano Key Topology along the North Coast

CAVEATS, SPECIAL INFORMATION, and HELPFUL HINTS

The North Coast of Scotland from Balnakiel Bay to Ceannabeinne Bay is written up as <u>Pebble Route 4</u> of the **North West Highlands Geopark Pebble Route Collection** (<u>www.nwhgeopark.com</u>).

The British Geological Survey has produced an excellent set of maps and materials about six different "Pebble Routes" you can take across the Highlands. Before the Scottish government in its wisdom closed all but two of its Visitor's Centers, it was possible to buy the "The Pebble Route Collection" and several other books and guides to the geology of the area. Now that the Visitor's Center's at Sango Bay has been closed, we will try our best to explain the geology you see here, but we know it will be a sorry substitute for the maps, displays, and personal knowledge once available from the people who used to staff the Visitor's Center.

Although the Visitor's Center in Durness is probably closed, the large specimens of the rocks from the area north coast were, as of early May 2019, still arrayed on the lawn. Looking at them will help you better understand the rocks we have been discussing in previous sections of this Guide. Taking photos of them will help you visualize the geological formations in this part of Scotland in ways that written descriptions cannot.

> **Directions to First Stop:** Continue driving on the A838. On the kyle (water)-side of the road, there are several small pull offs along the road. Choose any one.

KDC1: *'It's Not So Easy Being Green'*: The Kyle of Durness.

Location: OS Grid: NC 384656. If you're lucky, you will find yourself at Stop 13 on the Geopark Rock Route. If not, any view of the Kyle of Durness, especially at low tide is spectacular!

Web Sites: scotlandinfo.eu.

Discussion: There is one remarkable thing to note as you look around you and over the Kyle of Durness: it's GREEN! Green—that color you haven't seen since Elphin. A color you couldn't previously have described without the modifier "drab" in front of it.

The change in the color of the landscape around you tells you that there has been a dramatic change in the rocks. As you probably guessed, you have re-entered the world of those soft, life affirming Cambrian rocks you left behind along the north shore of Loch Assynt.

But wait there's more: if the tide is out, here you can also see some of the most extensive and interesting *mud flats* in the western Highlands.

KDC-1: The Extensive Mud Flats in the Kyle of Durness

It is only recently that mud flats have gained some of the geological respect they deserve, so we'll take a minute to point out what distinguishes them from other habitats:

1. Mud flats can exist only where they are protected from waves. Sand bars and low lying islands usually provide this protection, but other obstacles like piers can serve as well. However, if these barriers are removed or flooded, the mud flats will disappear.

2. In terms of elevation, "a little" means "a lot" on a mud flat. Mere inches of elevation make tremendous differences in habitat, and the life forms that live on it.

3. Phytoplankton (plants) and zooplankton (animals) are the most important inhabitants of a mud flat because they are the base of the food web. They are eaten by all the other life forms that live in, on and around the mud flat including worms, mud snails, shrimp, oysters, clams, mussels, crabs, fish, rays, birds, and us.

4. Because your home is inundated and dried out twice a day, toughness and adaptability are the keys to evolutionary success if you live on a mud flat. (Actually if you live anywhere.) [See Google: "mudflat food web."]

Cyanobacteria, the blue green algae you can see growing in the shallows and on the edges of ponds, here and everywhere else in the world, are the earth's oldest life form. And even today, we could not exist without them. Their job? Eating carbon and excreting oxygen. That's right, every breath you take is due to the metabolism of cyanobacteria. We owe everything to them, yet almost no one has ever heard of them. And those that have, think of them only by their common name: *pond scum*.

Unfortunately, although stromatolites are relatively common in Scotland, they are rare in the areas covered by this Guide. If you want to see them here, you will need to walk out to the outcrops on the south shore of Balnakiel Bay, along the cliffs below the golf course. (See KDC-3.) [For a description of the outcrops along the south shore of Balnakiel Bay, see Excursion 14 in Goodenough and Krabbendam. Also see: "Stromatolites" at fossilmuseaum.net.]

> **Directions:** To drive to Balnakeil Bay, turn west (left) at the (only) intersection in Durness. Drive through the Balnakeil Craft Village, follow the road around to the right, and park in the parking areas near the ruins of the church and around the golf course entrance.

KDC-2: 'Mylonites, You've Got the Cutest Little Mylonites!' The Metamorphic Rocks of Balnakiel Bay

Location: Balnakiel Bay, west of Durness. Walk down to the beach or look over the beach from the car park at the very dark rocks cropping out along the shore.

92

KDC-2: Mylonites at Balnakiel Bay

Discussion: The dark rocks partially buried in the sand and scattered around the beach below the parking area are **mylonites** created by the extreme heat and pressure generated by the Moine thrust as it was riding over the (now) Cambrian rocks. The stress and pressure that the thrust put on those rocks was so great that they their internal crystal lattices failed and the molecules later) recrystallized- "metamorphosed"- into the mylonites you see here. This recrystallizing affected not just the soft Cambrian sedimentary rocks but the much harder, already re-crystallized Precambrian Lewisian gneisses beneath them as well.

Mylonites are called "oystershell rocks" for the obvious reason--they look as if they are made of piles of broken up oyster shells. But, unlike piles of real oyster shells, mylonite "crystals" are so tightly welded together it is almost impossible to pry them apart.

Mylonites tell us of the presence of thrust faults because no other force can recrystallize rock without melting it into magma. In other words, if you find mylonites, you find thrust faults, a fact which makes mylonites a structural geologist's, if not the original rocks, best friend.

> **Directions to Next Stop:** Drive to the parking area of what used to be the Durness Visitors Center and park. Although the Visitor's Center is now closed, large "samples" of the rock units you have been reading about in this Guide are displayed on the lawn. Here you can see in detail rocks you have mostly seen at a distance or, much smaller in size at the rock wall at Knockan Crag. It is worth looking at them closely.
>
> After you have finished looking at the exemplar rocks, walk down to Sango Beach. Please follow established paths and try to avoid the grassy area which is a very small and fragile machair which does not need to be walked on. Walk to the northwest end of the beach to the headland of dark rocks that forms the northwest end of the bay. You are looking for a section along the rock face that is above head height
>
> Note the pink colored rocks along the shoreline, then the dark rocks above them, then a small whitish out crop about 40 feet above the beach that resembles the profile of a jowly faced man with his mouth open. In this case, the term "cliff face" will take on new meaning.

KDC-3. *"He Been Having Some Far Travelin'"*: The Old Man in the Outcrop (with apologies to Woody Guthrie)

Location: Sango Bay, Durness. NC 4080 6770-to 4070 6800. N58 34 04, W4 44 24. This is one of the most beautiful beaches in a land full of beautiful beaches. It is best seen on walks! Take time to enjoy it!

Web Sites: "walkhighlands.co.uk" and "Ceannabeinne" at [revolvy.com]

Discussion: As you walk the beach, note the pink colored rocks cropping out under the black rocks along the headlands. This is a *pegmatite*, an igneous rock very similar to granite but with larger crystals. It has been pushed up (intruded) into the already existing Durness limestones. The presence of "intrusive" rocks like granites always indicates **crustal extension** or lengthening of the earth's crust, at the time they were intruded.

On the other hand, the dark rocks scattered along the beach are *mylonites*, close relatives of our old friends from Balnakiel Bay (KDC-1). Mylonites always indicate the presence of thrust faults, the earth's "go to" strategy for **crustal shortening**. Above the mylonites, and sometimes the pegmatites, are the very dark colored Durness carbonates, which were the victims of all this pushing together and pulling apart. And just above the dark Durness limestones, about 20-30 feet above the sand, is a small but fascinating geological 'formation' that looks a bit like a face.

KDC-3: The Old Man in the Cliff Face at Sango Beach

Here you are again looking at a thrust fault, but this time it is looking back at you! So, reading the rock units you see in this photo, from the beach ↑upwards↑, as things are done in geology, the rock units and geologic events are:

<u>Rock Unit D.</u>—Moine mylonites which show as dark, thinly bedded rocks at the top of the outcrop.

Thrust Fault 2, the Moine Thrust, which shows in the noticeable break in slope between the dark Moine mylonites (above) and the light colored rocks immediately below.

<u>Rock Unit C.</u>—The "far travelled Quartzites that form the "cliff face" (we can't make this stuff up) and show up here as grayish to whitish rocks. The eyes and the lips look white in this photo. But, even though they are in the right place in the section, lab analyses of the rocks themselves have shown that they do not match our old friend the Basal Quartzites. So they are not the same quartzites you saw at Loch Assynt.

But whose quartzites are they and where did they come from? No one seems to know, or Corky hasn't found the article that has definitively established this. So we have to go with the most probable—as amazing as this will sound: These quartzites were torn off an outcrop somewhere in central Scotland and carried here on a thrust fault that predated the Moine thrust. In honor of this amazing feat, and in full defiance of the naming conventions of the Stratigraphic Code, the rocks have been named the "Far Travelled Quartzites!"

Thrust Fault 1. The unnamed thrust fault which carried the Far Travelled Quartzites here. It shows up as the break in slope just under the Old Man's collar--the break in slope just under grayish as light-reddish rubble and looks a little like a clown's bow tie, immediately below the face.

<u>Rock Unit B.</u> —Durness limestones which show as the dark grey, iron stained, thickly bedded rocks that extend down to the sand.

<u>Rock Unit A.</u>—The pink colored pegmatites in the sand.

KDC-4: The Pegmatite Intrusion into the Durness Limestone

If you are lucky enough to be able to stay in the Durness area for a few hours or days, be sure to look at the Old Man under different lighting conditions. You will be amazed at how much his expressions seem to change. And, if nothing else, this outcrop proves that there is a lot that geologists still don't know even about one of the most famous and most studied geological sites in the world! Or, put another way, it shows that geology can be fun!

Directions: From Sango Bay, drive East toward Smoo Cave, watching carefully for white rocks that have fallen on the berm and a small turn out on your right (south). Pull into this turnout as far as you can. A small quarry of quartzites is on your right. You may be able to walk into the quarry but if you cannot, pick up one small piece of float to examine.

KDC-4. *And You Thought You'd Seen the Last of Them:* The "Basal" Quartzites Return

Location: A small quarry on the right hand side of the road, one mile east of Sango Sands.

Note: You must not drop anything into the sump. Not only could you block it, causing untold problems; but you would be reliving a rather unpleasant and macabre episode in the cave's history: in the late 17th century, a local and infamous highwayman named MacMurdo is believed to have killed as many as 20 people and hidden his crimes by dropping their bodies into this sink hole. True or not, nothing more needs to be added now.

Discussion: Our old friends the "basal" quartzites have returned to road level where we can see them in a quarry along the road and, as shown in the following photograph, at the fenced off area where the water of the Alt Smoo enters the Cave. Because they are more resistant to weathering and erosion than the limestones and dolostones, the quartzites that are "re-engineering" the recent growth and configuration of the Cave!

Illustration KDC-4 shows the "sump" in the quartzites through which the waters of the Alt Smoo gush into the Cave. We were fortunate to be visiting on a day when they had diverted the water for maintenance. Normally it is roaring loudly from the water gushing through it.

KDC-4: The (dry) Smoo Cave Sump in the Quartzites

Since the limestones in the Cave weather so much more readily than the quartzites, the likely fate of Smoo Cave is that it will continue to erode the limestones laterally along the quartzite boundary. So the waterfalls inside the Cave may become wider but the cave will not extend much further back into the hillside because the quartzites are so much more resistant to weathering than the dolostones. This should make for higher and wider waterfalls in a cave not much deeper than Smoo Cave is now. Be sure to come back in a thousand years or so and see.

Directions to Next Stop: Return to your car and drive east to the Smoo Cave parking lot, about a mile east. The entrance to the parking lot is well marked and there is usually space to park. Before you go to the cave itself, read the Interpretive Panels, which are excellent. Note that while everyone can visit the outer sections of the Cave, the innermost chamber is accessible only by "pay-to-ride" boat tours. If you want to walk down to the Caves, note that there are some steep slopes and lots of stairs. Both can be slippery when wet, and this being Scotland it is almost always wet. And, of course, it's even wetter inside the cave! So wear good, preferably waterproof boots and a jacket or rain slicker. Bring your walking stick and some water. Believe it or not, despite all the water that will be dripping on and around you, you will get thirsty. The round trip down to and through the Cave will take a minimum of 30 minutes.

KDC-5: *Are There Any Shmoos Left In Smoo Cave?* : A Triple Treat Cave!

Location: NC 418 671. Smoo Cave, Scotland @ geologypage.com.

Discussion: "Schmoos" were small, mysterious, bowling pin shaped creatures that were featured in Al Capp's cartoons in the late 1940's through the '50's. (You can read all about them by entering "shmoo" in Wiki.)

Alas for all of us who grew up a thousand years ago reading Li'l Abner cartoons that featured those delightful creatures the *schmoos*, Smoo Cave was not named for them. Instead, the name **"smoo"** probably came from the Norse words *smjugg* or *smuga*, and meant a "hole" or "hiding-place." *Hidden cave* is probably as good a translation and description as any!

Smoo Cave is large as caves go: 200 feet long, 130 feet wide at its widest point, and 50 feet high at the entrance. It is one of the few caves in the world that hits a "triple double!" It is:

(1) a *quartzite cave* **and** a *dolostone cave*,

(2) a *chemically* **and** a *mechanically* weathered cave, **as well as**

(3) a *sea cave* and a *fresh water cave*—all linked in one dynamic system.

Taking these in order as you walk through the cave, (1) The front part of the Cave is composed of *dolostone*, a type of limestone made of magnesium carbonate. The back part of the Cave is composed of *quartzite*, aka cemented sand. (2) Dolostones are softer and weather (dissolve) more readily in wet environments. Quartzites are harder and more resistant to chemical weathering but more susceptible to abrasive weathering. This is why the softer dolostones have "retreated" back to the quartzites. (3) The northern end of the Cave is open to the sea, making it, duh, a sea cave and susceptible to wave erosion, while the southern end is a fresh water cave that is affected by the effects of rain and ground water. The nodules you see "littering" the floor of the cavern are quartzite nodules that have weathered out of the limestones.

As you approach the rear of the cave, you will hear and see the stream (the Alt Smoo) gushing over a 66 foot (20m) high waterfall. This change occurs at the dolostone-quartzite contact and shows how much more resistant to weathering the quartzites are than the dolostone under these conditions. The elongated blobs you see "littering" the floor of the cavern are **chert nodules** that have weathered out of the dolostone. Archaeologists have also found Neolithic, Iron Age and Norse artifacts in the Cave, testifying to its long history of human use. And much of that history was violent. The name **smoo** probably comes from the Norse word "smuga" which means "hole" or "hiding place," testifying perhaps to a long history of piracy and violence.

The stream, called the Alt Smoo, flows from a sink hole on the surface outside the cave. After you leave the Cave and climb back up to the Visitors Center, walk along the road to the fenced in "sump", where the water enters the cave. The volume of water gushing through it is amazing!

Fun with Geology: You can "replicate" the evolution of Smoo Cave at dinner tonight! Order steak, mashed potatoes with gravy, and peas, please. (We know, a hardship but you must suffer for science!) Stir the a few peas into the mashed potatoes and push the mixture up against, but not over, the steak. Now pour the hot gravy slowly but steadily over the steak and potatoes. The steak is resistant to the gravy, like the quartzites, so the gravy just puddles up on top and drips down the sides, But the potato mixture is softer and less resistant to the gravy, so it 'washes away', leaving some "pea nodules: behind. This is called "playing with your food for science!" It's hard work but someone has to do it!

Directions to Last Stop: Return to your car and drive east to closest (westernmost) of the three parking area/overlooks above Cienbiennie Bay and overlooking Whitten Head to the east. Park.

KDC-6: *Play It Again, Finn*: **The 'Piano Key' Topography along the North Coast.**

Location: The westernmost of the three Cienbiennie Overlooks along the A838 west of the Smoo Cave Parking area.

Discussion: You can find a panoramic view of the Northwest Coast of Scotland from many vantage points along the road from Balnakiel Bay to the Cienbiennie Overlooks. Note that the sandy bays and beaches (Balnakeil, Sango Bay, and Ceanbiennie Bay) are divided by and sandwiched between narrow headlands that extend further out into the North Sea than the sandy beaches.

KDC-6: Horst and Graben Landforms indicative of Crustal Lengthening

Looking down at the beach below you and west across the headlands and beaches, it looks as if Finn, our friendly but easily frustrated giant, had been trying to make a piano for Oona, with the dark headlands—the slender black keys—and the sandy beaches-- the white keys. But the black keys kept sticking out too far above the white keys and the piano wouldn't play. So, in frustration, he hit the keyboard a couple times in frustration and stomped away! Such can be the temper of giants! And such can be the beauty they inadvertently leave in their wake.

Unfortunately for stories of frustrated giants, this type of landform is actually quite common. The Basin and Range Province in the American West is another example of it. It is called a *horst and graben structure*. The dark uplifted dark rocks are the *horsts* or headlands and the sandy beaches between them are the *grabens*. (*Horst* comes from the German word for "hedge" and *graben* from the German word for "ditch.")

In other words, horsts and grabens are blocks of earth that have been raised or lowered relative to each other, resulting in older rock units cropping out next to and often above younger units, as you see here. They occur when a land mass is being "stretched" (pulled apart laterally).

Horst and graben structures and igneous intrusions (the pink pegmatites you see along the beaches) always indicate periods of *crustal lengthening*. They are the opposite of thrust faulting, which shortens the crust. (The outcrops at Ullapool, Knockan Crag, and Unapool are evidence of thrust faulting.)

But, while it is not unusual to see thrust faults, horsts and grabens and igneous intrusions at many different locations around the world, it is very unusual is see them in the same place in real time. Being able not just to see from afar but to walk among such clear evidence of crustal lengthening and of crustal shortening--in the same place in real time-- is a geologist's dream!

Optional Side Trip 1: The Cambrian Succession Along The North Shore Of Balnakiel Bay

Section 14A of Goodenough and Krabbendam's **Geological Excursion Guide to the Northwest Highlands** describes this trip. It is rather a hike to get to the west end of the beach along the north shore of Balnakiel Bay. But, if you want to see the rocks of the famous "Cambrian Succession," that you saw at Loch Assynt but with clearer outcrops, this walk will do it. This area has been designated a Site of Special Scientific Interest (SSSI), so there is an interpretive panel at the Club House.

You can also see **stromatolites** at some locations on this trek. Stromatolites are fossilized layers of pond scum. Each generation of new pond scum lived on top of its own waste products—a not altogether unfamiliar life strategy. Over millions of years, cyanobacteria took over the Precambrian world, oxygenated the atmosphere, and prepared the way for animal life. And they are still with us. Colonies of stromatolites live today in Western Australia, Mexico, the Bahamas, and a few other shallow, calm oceanic environments.

Thus, as unassuming as they appear, stromatolites are the ancestors of all life on earth- past and present. Merely by metabolizing, over billions of years, they pumped enormous amounts of oxygen into the atmosphere, and thereby remade the earth's atmosphere.

However, as in any system, no resource goes unexploited for long. New life forms developed to feed on all that algae, and evolution was off and, if not running, at least multiplying and diversifying. Fittingly, we leave it to Malcolm Rider to have the final say: *The Precambrian is the evolution (or lack of it) of stromatolites and the cyanobacteria... There is no other life...until there was!*

Optional Side Trip 2. Cape Wrath

> **Warning: It may be illegal for a geologist or someone interested in geology to visit northern Scotland and not go out to Cape Wrath at least once! So, you should schedule your trip as soon as possible. You can book the ferry, which leaves from Keodale landing, at the MacKay Hotel in Durness.**

(Inquire locally, but note you may not be able to make reservations either for the ferry or for the hotel on short notice.)

However long you plan to spend on Cape Wrath, your visit will require planning. For example, if you want to see the view from the lighthouse, walk around a bit, and have a cuppa, the short time (usually around an hour) scheduled for you to be there will be long enough. But, if you want to walk the geology, get up close and personal with the amazing pegmatites, study the Scourie dike intrusions, and get a feel for the most remote place in Scotland, you will want to stay longer. And, to do that, you must make arrangements.

To visit Cape Wrath is to experience the earth at its most elemental. Here you are back at the beginning of time on this planet, touching the earth's very roots, and experiencing the powers of water and waves that shaped it. Malcolm Rider, a geologist who would probably hate being called a poet, says, nonetheless poetically, of Cape Wrath:

> *It is as though these rocks somehow contain the runes of life itself. There is certainly an essence (here)… a presence without there being one, a truth with there only being imagination…* (Rider, **Hutton's Arse**, p. 177).

END TRIP 6

HAIL AND FAREWELL!
The Ceannabeinne Overlooks
CBO

Directions: Drive 6.1 miles east of Durness on the A838 or about a 2 miles east of Smoo Cave. There are three pullouts along the road overlooking Ceannabeinne Bay. Start at the one furthest east and work your way back west toward Durness. When you have parked at the easternmost one, walk to the "Ceannabeinne Township Trail" Interpretive Panel on the north side of the road. Be very, very careful! Cars travelling from Tongue to Durness are coming out of a long steep incline and are rounding a left hand (to them) curve. They may not be looking for pedestrians along the highway, so you need to look out for them.

The horst and graben structures described in the previous section are particularly evident when you look west from this overlook.)

The walk down to the beach on the "Township Trail passes the ruins of what used to be a village of about 14 houses, one of which is still standing. But you can see the walls of the other houses and get a feel both for land and the effects of the Clearances that drove pople off it.

Location: 58.33.06N, 4.41.17W.

Discussion: *Ceannabeinne* means the "end of the mountains." We could not have found a better name or place for our last stop if we had ordered one from **Geosites-R-Us**. From here you can see:

1. Lewisian Gneiss (Europe's Oldest Rocks). The grey, hummocky hills below you and to the South are the by now familiar **Lewisian gneiss**, which is around 3 billion years old, making them not only the oldest rocks in Scotland but are among the oldest rocks in the world. Precambrian rocks similar to the Lewisian form the cores of all our current continents except Antarctica.

2. Granites. Granites are igneous rocks that cooled slowly enough while deep within the earth that large crystals had time to grow and were later lifted up to the surface. You saw them forming Fionnphort Harbor on Mull, and they are the pink rocks cropping out under the Durness limestones at Sango Beach. The intrusion of the pegmatites is the reason that the rocks forming the west shore of the beach, opposite you, are tilted vertically.

3. Schists. Schists are metamorphic rocks whose crystals have been realigned into platy, often silver looking sheets. You saw them on Mull and they crop out along the Moine thrust east of Whitten Head, the headlands to the East.

4. Scotland's Oldest Sedimentary Rocks. TheTorridonian rocks that you have seen at Ardmair and Loch Assynt and forming the mountains in the far distance are Scotland's oldest sedimentary rocks.

5. The Cambrian Succession. The "Basal Quartzites" that you saw at the small quarry at KDC-5, in Fingal's cave at KDC5, and along Loch Assynt are at the base of the "Cambrian Succession" which saw the beginnings of multicellular life on earth. The bright green swatches around Smoo Cave and Durness and in isolated patches elsewhere indicate the presence of limestones. Where you see green plants growing, you are probably looking at areas where the Durness limestones crop out on or near the earth's surface.

6. Beaches. Cienbiennie, Sango, and Balnakiel Beaches are among of the most beautiful and most photographed beaches in the British Isles. They may soon need to be protected from their own popularity.

7. Mylonites. Looking again to the west across toward Sango Bay, you can see outcrops of the "oyster shell" mylonites cropping out along the beach and faithfully pointing out the presence of thrust faults. (You saw

8. Thrust Faulting. Mylonites themselves are the best evidence of thrust faulting. If you look north to Faraid Head and west to Balnakiel Bay, you are looking at the end of the Moine thrust in this area. This moving of enormous blocks of earth up and over other blocs of earth results in crustal shortening.

9. Horst and Graben Topography. Across the North Coast from Cienbiennie to Cape Wrath, you can see the wide bays and beaches (Balnakeil Bay, Sango Bay, and Ceanbiennie Bay) divided by and sandwiched between dark, narrow, rocky "fingers" of land.

This is caused by blocs of earth being moved up or down relative to each other during episodes of *crustal lengthening*.

10. Machairs. If you walk down to Cienbiennie beach you will be crossing a small remnant *machair,* similar to the small one at Sango Beach and akin from afar to the much larger and better developed machair at Fidden Farms on Mull (see Mul-2).

11. The Effects of Human Activity. Now it's time to read the Interpretative Panel about the Scottish "Clearances" in the parking area and then follow the path down to the beach. The Clearances were acts of genocide that were so effective that today, more than only 10% of the population that lived here in 1800, lives here now.

In Gaelic, the Highland Clearances are called the *Fuadach nan Gaidheal,* the "Eviction of the Gael," a much better term than "Highland Clearances" which suggests the cleaning out of attics or the selling off unbought items. It lacks any connotation of the violence, greed, and self-dealing that characterized the actual, centuries long, systematic, and violent removal of thousands of **people** from the land on which they had lived on centuries. So we will use the term "eviction."

And "Gael," for its part, is a far better than the term "Highland." The Highlands are a geographic region. You have been travelling across a small part of it since you left Ullapool. And "Highlands" is a rather antiseptic way of referring to a place while not talking about its people. Using it in the context here obscures the fact that it was people and their animals who were evicted from land they had lived on for generations. So, however it has been dressed up in the rationales of the Scientific Agriculture Movement and the "necessities of progress," the "Eviction of the Gael" **was** cultural genocide. And the scattering of families and clans who had lived on the Highlands for hundreds of years **was** a Diaspora.

If the children of the Scottish Diaspora whom we meet at Scottish games and festivals in the States miss Scotland, the Highlands itself seem to miss its people. Many fewer people live here now than could. The machairs are dying, in part because humans no longer live on them and help maintain their complicated, interdependent ecosystem. Wind farms and golf courses tear up the land, destroy fragile habitats, and disrupt flyways while failing even to promote small settlements to grow up around them. "Gated" communities deny access to what were once common lands. We could go on, but we are hardly innocent ourselves: we flew here in airplanes and have driven—and are encouraging you to drive—all over the Highlands, expending the planets very limited gas and oil resources on sightseeing. If the geology of the Highlands tells us anything, it is that even small "causes," like stromatolites and pipe worms, can have far reaching, long term "effects", which we likely do not fully understand and probably cannot foresee.

Despite these melancholy notes, we do hope that by following this Guide and learning about Scotland's fascinating and unique geology, you have acquired an appreciation for Scotland that you did not have before. And in doing so, have gained a deeper appreciation of the amazing and ever changing story of our planet.

12. Glacial Erratics. Along the near skyline to the southwest large, oddly shaped boulders dot the skyline. These are **erratics**—rocks from other places that were carried along by glaciers and dumped here as the glaciers melted.

A "family" of glacial erratics silhouetted against the evening sky.

The erratics are composed of Lewisian gneiss, making this a photograph of, simultaneously, the oldest and the youngest rocks in Scotland. It seems a fitting image to end these Guides and to wish you both beauty and endurance.

BIBLIOGRAPHY

books

Baxter, Stephen. **Ages in Chaos: James Hutton and the Discovery of Deep Time.** 2003. New York: Tom Doherty Associates, A Forge Book.

Carroll, Sean. **From Eternity to Here: The Quest for the Ultimate Theory of Time.** (2010) New York: Penguin Books.

Friend, Peter. **Scotland: Looking at the Natural Landscapes.** (2012) London: HarperCollins.

Goodenough, Kathryn M. and Krabbendam, Maarten. **A Geological Excursion Guide to the North-West Highlands of Scotland.** (2011) Edinburgh: British Geological Survey.

Jones, Rosalind. **Mull in the Shaping** and **Mull in the Making.** (Continuous Printings since 1997) (www. Craigmore-publications.co.uk)

Lyle, Paul. **The Abyss of Time: A Study in Geological Time and Earth History.** (2016) Edinburgh: Dunedin Academic Press Ltd.

MacDougall, Doug. **Why Geology Matters: Decoding the Past, Anticipating the Future.** (no date) London: University of California Press.

McIntyre, Donald and McKirdy, Alan. **James Hutton: Founder of Geology.** (2012) Perth, Scotland: National Museums of Scotland.

McKirdy, Alan. **Set in Stone: The Geology and Landscapes of Scotland. (**2015) Edinburgh: Birlinn, Ltd.

McKirdy, Alan, Gordon, John; and Crofts, Roger. **Land of Mountain and Flood: The Geology and Landforms of Scotland**. 2010. Edinburgh: Birlinn, Ltd.

McKirdy, Alan and Crofts, Roger. **Scotland: The Creation of its Natural Landscape**. (1999) Scottish Natural Heritage: Redgorton, Perth.

Montgomery, David R. **The Rocks Don't Lie**. (2012). London: W.W. Norton and Co.

Palmer, Douglas. **A History of the Earth in 100 Groundbreaking Discoveries**. (2011) Buffalo, NY: Firefly Book Ltd.

Rider, Malcolm. **Hutton's Arse: 3 Billion Years of Extraordinary Geology in Scotland's Highlands**. (2005) Rogert. Sutherland, Scotland: Rider-French Consulting Ltd.

Stone, P. **Bedrock Geology UK North: An explanation of the bedrock geology map of Scotland, northern England, Isle of Man and Northern Ireland.** (2008) Keyworth, Nottingham: British Geological Survey.

Strachan, Rob, Clark Friend, Ian Alsop, and Miller, Suzanne. **An Excursion Guide to the Moine: Geology of the Northern Highlands of Scotland**. (2010) Edinburgh: NMS Enterprises Limited.

Tait, Charles. **The North Coast 500 Guide Book**. (2017) Orkney: Tait Publishing Ltd.

Toghill, Peter. **The Geology of Great Britain: An Introduction. (**2013) Wiltshire, England: Crowood Press LTD.

RESOURCES FOR YOUTH

Cassidy, John. "Earth: A Wet, Dirty, Bumpy Rock." **Earthsearch: A Kid's Geography Museum in a Book.** (1993) Klutz Press: Palo Alto, Canada.

Hall, Cally and O'Hara, Scarlett (sic): **Earth Facts.** (1995) London, New York, Stuttgart: Dorling Kindersley.

Wilson, John. 2003. **"Dancing Elephants and Floating Continents": The Story of Canada Beneath Your Feet.** Key Porter Books Limited, Toronto, Canada.

BRITISH GEOLOGICAL SURVEY MAPS

British Geological Survey. **Bedrock Geology UK North 5th Edition** (2007).

British Geological Survey. **Scotland Special Sheet: Assynt (**2007).

British Geological Survey **Scotland Sheet 101E: Ullapool** (2013).

Ordnance Survey. OS Landranger Map 9: Cape Wrath, Durness & Scourie (2008).

PAMPHLETS and GUIDES

Guide to the North West Highlands UNESCO Global Geopark" at *www.Knockan-crag.co.uk*. (Accessed Summer 2017).

"Knockan Crag (with) Rock Route Map." Scottish Natural Heritage [Print brochure obtained Summer 2015].

"Know the Code Before You Go." Scottish Natural Heritage. Electronic brochure available at pubs@snh.gov.uk. [Print brochure obtained Summer 2015.]

"Visit Tadhail." Knockan Crag, National Nature Reserve. Scotland's National Nature Reserves. www.knockan-crag.co.uk.

"Cape Wrath: Moine, Eriboll, Durness & Balnakiel." [Print brochure obtained Summer 2015].

Printed in the United States
By Bookmasters